"BARACK OBAMA" OPERATION

by

Mikhail Kryzhanovsky

MIRACLAIRE PUBLISHING LLC
Kansas City, (MO) USA

Website: *www.miraclairepublishing.com*
Email: *info@miraclairepublishing.com*

P.O. Box 8616
Yaounde, Cameroon

ISBN-13: 978-0615980751
ISBN-10: 0615980759

Printed in the United States of America

Miraclaire Publishing makes every effort to ensure the accuracy of all the information ("Content") in its publications. However, Miraclaire and its agents and licensors make no representations or warranties whatsoever as to the accuracy, completeness, or suitability for any purpose of the Content and disclaim all such representations and warranties, whether expressed or implied to the maximum extent permitted by law. Any views expressed in this publication are the views of the author and are not necessarily the views of Miraclaire.

Democracy is not the power of people.
It's the power of Democrats.

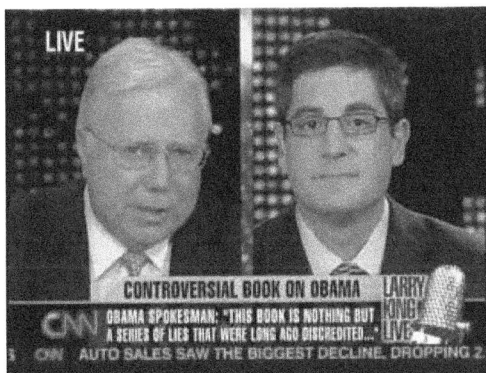

Jerry Corsi (l.), the author of "Where is the Birth Certificate?" and Obama's personal enemy: "Mike Kryzhanovsky, thank you for your courage".

My friend Corsi was a member of Mitt Romney-2012 team. Romney got this book from him, but he was too stupid to use it against Obama during 2012 presidential campaign. That's why he lost.

USSR foreign passport with US Visa

CONTENTS

**People involved in Operation "Barack Obama"
and "Mikhail Kryzhanovsky case"**

1. Vladimir Putin, President of Russia.
2. Mikhail Fradkov, SVR Director.
3. Barack Obama, the U.S. President
4. Bill Clinton, a former U.S. President
5. George W. Bush, a former U.S. President
6. Hillary Clinton, the U.S. Secretary of State
7. Janet Napolitano, the U.S. Homeland Security Secretary
8. Chuck Schumer, the U.S. Senator (D.-NY)
9. Kirsten Gillibrand, the U.S. Senator (D.-NY)
10. Patrick Fitzerald, the U.S. Special Counsel
11. CIA Directors: John Deutch, George Tenet, Porter Goss, Michael Hayden, Leon Panetta, David Petraeus.
12. Robert Mueller, FBI Director in 2001-2013
13. Mark Sullivan, the U.S. Secret Service Director in 2

INTRODUCTION
How They Protect Us

We'll talk here a lot about big politics and espionage, but I'd like to start with two most important things for everybody - war and peace, death and life.

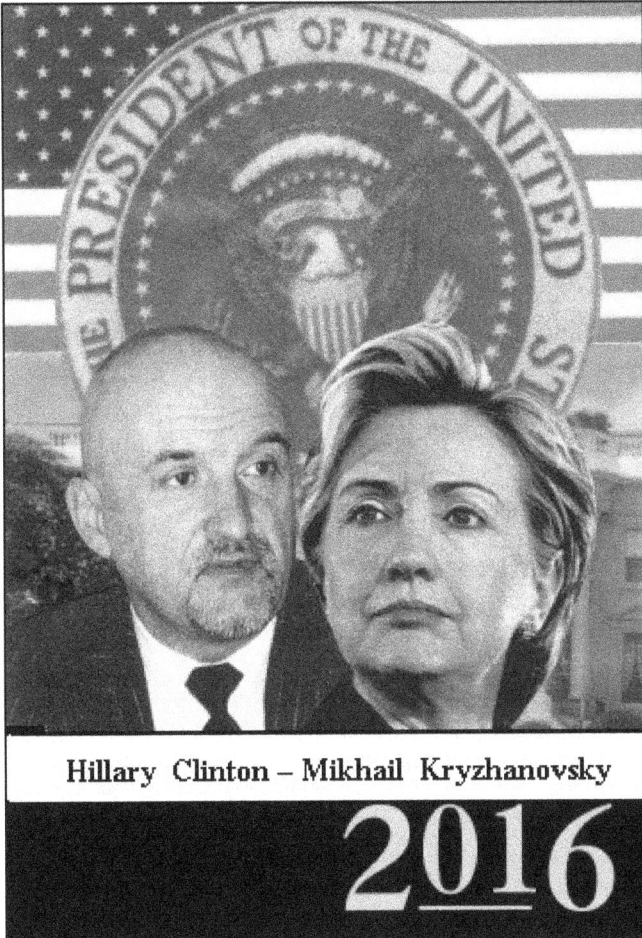

Hillary Clinton – Mikhail Kryzhanovsky

2016

Hillary helped me in 2002, I'm ready to help her in 2016 to win presidency, kick Obama out of the Oval Office and stop World War III [for Russia's resources - M.K.]. Otherwise, a Russian spy "Obama", pushed by Rockefellers and Rothchilds will have no choice but start the war and Americans will re-elect him again, no matter what the US Constitution says. With whom? Against whom? Just look at these superpowers with the biggest military budgets 2013:

1. USA - $ 582.4 bl.
2. China - 139.4 bl.
3. Russia - 68 bl.

How much time left if the war "prize" is Russia? By 2016 Russia will increase its military budget up to $ 98 bl, by 2020 they will finish their army total rearmament Program making the war impossible. Besides, Obama's job is to destroy America's economy as soon as possible.
Remember: "Obama" is a Communist. With Communists the trick is - once they get the power, they keep it forever.

You have to read this book to understand what's going on in the White House and what to stop the dictator do to save America. I know the truth and I'm ready to share. CIA, FBI and Secret Service tried to shut me up. My wife got a stroke after the Secret Service death squad broke into her apartment looking for me, two years later she died.

They can kill me, but I'll never surrender.

1st "Protection" Line
U.S. National Security Strategy 2010
(Ultimate stupidity)

1. Globalization intensified the dangers we face - international terrorism..."
   Wrong. International terrorism does not exist. Every group has a target of its own - mainly USA and Israel.

2. Renew our focus on Afghanistan as part of commitment to disrupt, dismantle and defeat al-Qa'ida.
   Wrong. 10 years - we got nothing; there's nothing to renew.

3. We must pursue a strategy of global leadership.

Wrong. We can't do it unless Russia and China are disintegrated as multinational states.

4. Our rejection of actions like tortures..."

Wrong. If CIA is not professional, if it has no damned secret sources what else they have to do ?

5. Key centers of influence - China, India, Russia [all - nuclear states)

Wrong. Obama is going to exclude USA from the superpowers' group by cutting the US nuclear arsenal - it's statistics.

6. We will pursue engagement with hostile nations [Iran and North Korea] to test their intentions.

Wrong. They are a threat to us, because we are not a threat to them.

7. Peace between Israel and his neighbors...

Wrong Peace is not profitable for both sides over there.

8. We must maintain our military conventional superiority, while enhancing its capacity to defeat assymetric threats.

Wrong. Army can't fight assymetric threats like guerrilla; it's all about intelligence special ops.

9. Our intelligence and homeland security efforts must be integrated with our security policies, and those of our allies...

Wrong. France, Germany and Israel are into industrial espionage in America.

10. Nations must have incentives to behave responsibly, or be isolated when they do not.

Wrong. Religious nations take punishment as a test.

11. Rebalance our military capabilities to excel at counter-terrorism, counterinsurgency, stability operations.

Wrong. WE have to rebalance our political efforts and redirect Taliban to other targets (countries).

12. Analysts, agents and officers who protect us must have access to all relevant intelligence throughout the government.

Very wrong. Imagine a 'mole" with such access!

And I would like to add:

14. The best workers (servants) for the West and USA are people from India, because they accept social inequality absolutely.

15. New world order will be established as a result of the World War III - 50% of the world population will be eliminated as there's not enough food and water on Earth. Then the world is going to have about 100-200 centers (a net) with good living conditions and "the rest of the world". You have to obey, otherwise they send you to "the other territory".

Why the West needs Russia

The Brookings Institution – London School of Economics "Project on Internal Displacement", September 2011

The project is about climate changes and possible relocation the population of the Pacific island. But it's actually about relocation of millions of Europeans to Russia (precisely - to Siberia which has vast lands with a small population and countless natural resources) in the next 10-15 years. The reason is predicted by science huge and catastrophic climate changes in 2000-2033 on Earth, never seen before earthquakes and hurricanes. Russia's territory will be safe and that's why it's so important to turn this country into the colony of the West as soon as possible.

2nd "Protection" Line
National Intelligence Strategy, 2005
(Why it does not work)

1. "At its core, this National Intelligence Strategy capitalizes on the extraordinary talents and patriotism of America's diverse intelligence professionals".
    Wrong. War in Iraq, which is a complete intelligence failure because of non-stop everyday terror, proves that we do not have any damned "extraordinary" intelligence talents.

2. "Strategic objectives. Develop innovative ways to penetrate and analyze the most difficult targets".
    Wrong. Innovative intelligence ways do not exist. You penetrate by recruiting a "mole" or through insider.

3. "Explore alternative analytic views".
    Wrong. True analysts have only one view, and it's the right one.

4. "Developing new methodologies…"
    Wrong. They do not exist.

5. "Analysis must do more than just describe what is happening and why; it must identify a range of opportunities for (and likely consequences of) diplomatic, military, law enforcement, or homeland security action".
    Wrong. Intelligence information has to be sent to State, Defense, Justice or Homeland Security Department – let them analyze, calculate opportunities, and take responsibility for the consequences.

6. "Make attention to long-term and strategic analysis a part of every analyst's assigned responsibilities."
    Wrong. Strategic analysis is a job for a very few.

7. "The Intelligence Community must foster cross-agency collaboration at all-levels".

Wrong. It's a Christmas gift for "moles".

8. "Expand the reporting of information of intelligence value from…private sector stakeholders".
  Wrong. It's a perfect opportunity for disinformation and our enemies will be happy to use it.

9. "Remove impediments to information sharing within the Community, and establish policies that reflect need-to-share (versus need-to-know) for all data, removing the "ownership" by agency of intelligence information".
  Wrong. Who put forward this idea? Another "mole"? "Need–to-know" is the only more or less effective security tool. Just give me the name – whose idea is that?

10. "Ensure the various Intelligence Community elements conducting counterintelligence activities act as a cohesive whole to undertake aggressive, unified counterintelligence operations".
  Wrong. Another gift for the "moles".

11. "Create a lessons-learned function to assess the effectiveness of the Community's activities as a "system of systems" in supporting national security goals".
  Wrong. That's a science fiction.

12. "The Intelligence Community must manage its resources by examining national security priorities, both short and long term".
  Wrong. All national security priorities, including war on terror, WMD proliferation and homeland security, are long term ones.

3rd "Protection" Line
National Counterintelligence Strategy of the United States 2007 (Why it does not work)

1. "The United States faces substantial challenges to its security, freedom and prosperity. Transnational terrorism, continued

proliferation of weapons of mass destruction (WMD), asymmetric warfare, extremist movements, and failed states present severe challenges to a just and stable world".

Wrong. Transnational terrorism does not exist.

2. "Subversion, treason and leaks expose our vulnerabilities, our governmental and commercial secrets, and our intelligence sources and methods. This insider threat has been a source of extraordinary damage to U.S. security. Countering this threat will require an aggressive national effort. [We] must develop new methods.... For example, electronic systems designed to discover unexplained patterns of activities or anomalous events".

Wrong. New counterespionage methods do not exist. I don't see how "aggressive national effort" could help you find a single "mole".

3. "No counterintelligence official can guarantee our nation will never suffer another incident of treason or espionage. We can, however, assure the President, the Congress, and the American people that we have measurably increased the rigor of our system of national intelligence, and we have put in place systems, practices, and procedures that make foreign penetration more difficult to accomplish and easier to detect".

Wrong. What "systems, practices and procedures"" are you talking about if Russians pay millions?

4. "We will also provide strategic analysis to the National Security Council".

Wrong. They don't need your strategic analysis. They need the "moles" names.

5. "The armed forces' effectiveness depends on their ability to conduct military operations uncompromised by adversaries' foreknowledge. The obligation to support such operations extends beyond the Defense Department to the entire counterintelligence community".

Wrong. Exchange of classified information within government agencies is a huge problem, because it's all about security of secret sources. I'm absolutely against this practice.

6. "The increasing complexity of counterintelligence challenges"
   Wrong. They are the same for the last one hundred years.

PART 1

PANDORA'S BOX

CHAPTER 1
Hitler, Gestapo Mueller and "Roosevelt Operation"

1939-1945, World War II
1. In May 1940, Germans surrounded 400 000 British troops at the French port of Dunkirk and 200 000 more - at other ports. Hitler ordered to stop Kleist's Tank Army, ready to slaughter half a million Brits and end up the British Empire. He also ordered Göring to stop airstrikes. He saved the enemy, allowing them to flee to Great Britain. No explanation.

2. In 1941, he appointed Goering his successor. No explanation.

3. On June 22, 1941 Hitler attacked the USSR. On July 1, 1941 he stopped the tank forces at Moscow suburbs and refocused the direction of the main attack to the south. No explanation.

4. In 1942, Hitler began to destroy the German economy - he ordered Martin Bormann to transfer Reichsbank funds to offshore companies. The order was a top secret.

5. On March 19, 1945, Hitler ordered to terminate the German industry, communications and transport (to end the war, of course). Albert Speer, the Minister of Armaments, managed to sabotage the order and Germans kept fighting for a month and a half.

6. Hitler's fate is unknown:
  - allegedly committed suicide by taking cyanide
  - allegedly committed suicide - shot himself
  - allegedly was shot
  - allegedly KGB exhumed corpses and identified Hitler and Eva Braun
  - allegedly their bodies were buried on the territory of the Soviet military base in Magdenburge, East Germany, and in 1970 KGB Chairman Y. Andropov ordered to burn the bodies. Why?

Now, something absolutely impossible -Stalin did not even bother to find Hitler, dead or alive - official order doesn't exist! A small KGB team arrived from Moscow for 1 (one) day, looked at Führer's bunker and... left.
 Hitler was a KGB asset?

October, 1995

Millennium Hilton, New York

At secret CIA headquarters (room 3111, Millennium Hilton, New York) I discussed with CIA agents Gestapo methods. Actually, I wanted to find Gestapo Chief Mueller who disappeared in May, 1945. He was fully in charge and thus responsible to execute the extermination of the Jews of Europe. The CIA agents got very angry: "We don't recommend you to do this. Stop it!" I want international Jewish community to ask the White House what it means.

Note. "The head of the Jewish section of the Gestapo (IVB), Obersturmannfuerer Eichman, estimated in his report that 2,000,000 Jews had been killed by shooting mainly by the Eintzatz Groups. This did not include the estimated 4,000,000

sent by the Gestapo for extermination in annihilation camps"
.The International Military Tribunal, Nurnberg, 1946, Volume II,
Chapter XV, p.282"

Killing of Jews at Ivangorod and in Vinnitsa, Ukraine 1942

June 13, 1942
The Office of Strategic Services was established by a Presidential
military order issued by President Roosevelt.

November 28- December 1, 1943

Stalin, Roosevelt, Churchill   Otto Scorzeny

Maya Mykota   Lida Lisovsky

Stalin, Roosevelt and Churchill met at Tehran to plan the final strategy for the war against Nazi Germany and its allies, and the chief discussion was centered on the opening of a second front in Western Europe. German intelligence had learned of the conference in mid-October 1943, after breaking a US Navy cod. Hitler wasn't really interested (why – see Ch. 2) but he had to approve the "Long Jump" operation headed by SS-Obersturmbannfuhrer (Lieutenant Colonel) Otto Scorzeny. KGB first became aware of the plot from two secret agents,sisters and prostitutes – Maya Mikota and Lida Lisovsky. Mikota got her German boyfriend SS Sturmbannfuhrer Hans Ulrich von Ortel to tell her the following:" I have to go for a month and I'll bring you a beautiful Persian carpet - we never made love on the carpet".

Six German radio operators were dropped by parachute and made their way to Tehran, but were eventually found by Soviet agents led by Gevork Vartanian. The operation was called off; Skorzeny himself considered the intelligence coming from Tehran to be inadequate and did not believe the complex scheme could have worked. Roosevelt lived in Soviet Embassy for security reasons and they became friends with Stalin, especially after KGB got a very rare stamp for Roosevelt who was a very serious philatelist. They even talked in private about the possibility of the Soviet-American Peace and Friendship Treaty. American big business which was making big money on World War II and already planning future Cold War against Soviet Union got information about the talks – Roosevelt had to die.

1942 - 1945

Heinrich Mueller   **Bill Donovan, OSS Chief**

Gestapo Chief Heinrich Mueller was recruited and worked for Office of Strategic Services (OSS). At OSS order he planned and executed the operation to poison the US President Franklin Roosevelt. He was last seen in the Führerbunker in Berlin on May 1, 1945, the day after Hitler's suicide. The CIA's file on Muller was released under the Freedom of Information. Act in 2001, and documents several unsuccessful attempts by U.S. agencies to find Mueller. The U.S. National Archives commentary on the file concludes: "Though inconclusive on Muller's ultimate fate, the file is very clear on one point. The CIA and its predecessors (OSS) did not know Muller's whereabouts at any point after the war. The CIA was never in contact with Mueller."

April 12, 1945
On the afternoon of April 12, Roosevelt said, "I have a terrific pain in the back of my head." He then slumped forward in his chair, unconscious, and was carried into his bedroom. The president's attending cardiologist, Dr. Bruenn, diagnosed a massive cerebral hemorrhage (stroke). At 3:35 pm Roosevelt died. Three American presidents - Harry Truman, Dwight Eisenhower and John Kennedy rejected Roosevelt family's request for autopsy - they knew who killed the President, they knew about Mueller and nobody wanted to be next.

June 4, 1961
During a short brake in Vienna Summit between John Kennedy and Soviet Premier Nikita Khruschhev, Kennedy's Press Secretary Pier Sallinger, introduced to the President Soviet journalist Valentin Zorin who asked why Kennedy refused the autopsy of Roosevelt's body. Kennedy got angry: "I'll OK the autopsy and there might be traces of a poison. It won't bring Roosevelt back but what people would think about the country where they poison presidents like rats?"

President Ronald Reagan and Valentin Zorin

Nazi hunters give up?
October 12, 2011
Efraim Zuroff, Head, Simon Wiesenthal Centre
1 Mendele Street, Jerusalem, 92147, Israel
swcjerus@netvision.net.il
Dear Mr Zuroff,
In May, 2010 I've sent you the evidence that Gestapo Chief Mueller worked for CIA and asked you for investigation into the case. I insist on any answer from you, a prominent Nazi hunter. Thank you. Mikhail Kryzhanovsky

October 19, 2011
I've talked to Melissa Hooper, New York Simon Wiesenthal Office (212-697-1293) on the case. She said they tried to get anything from CIA on Mueller and got nothing at all. They appreciate my help but they are just tired. Hey, what are you going to do about this, Mr. Benjamin Netanyahu, the Prime Minister of Israel?

CHAPTER 2
CIA Operation "John Kennedy"

September 18, 1947
The National Security Act of 1947 established the CIA. The agency conducts covert operations and paramilitary actions, and exerts foreign political influence through its Special Activities Division.

August 5, 1962

Robert Kennedy, Marilyn Monroe, John Kennedy

CIA agents killed Marilyn Monroe (staged suicide - "acute barbiturate poisoning") who got information on planned JFK assassination and desperately tried to contact him or his brother, Robert Kennedy. It's simple to kill without any traces on or in the body – use a suppository.

November 22, 1963
President John Kennedy was assassinated at 12:30 p.m.in Dealey Plaza, Dallas, Texas.

President Kennedy shot.

What's conspiracy? It's when you ask the government a simple question and nobody wants to answer it. And if you ask the wrong questions you get the wrong answers, as with the Warren Commission. Let's ask some good questions.

Question 1. What would have happened if the snipers missed the target or Kennedy survived, being merely wounded - sniper is a human being - he makes mistakes.
Answer. Kennedy would have won the 1964 Presidential election and then conceivably his brothers, Robert and Edward, would keep the Oval Office until 1984 (count the years for yourself). No war in Vietnam. The CIA would have been shut down. The FBI and Pentagon would have been "cleaned up" and "cleaned out."

Question 2. Why would the CIA, FBI and big business behind them, not to mention others who had their eye on the Oval Office, take such a huge risk?
Answer. There was no risk at all and there was no "huge conspiracy - there was a "passive sabotage" operation. CIA Director John McCone, FBI Director Edgar Hoover and Secret Service Director James Rowley made a deal not to touch Lee Harvey Oswald until operation is over.

Kennedy, Dulles, McCone   Edgar Hoover   James Rowley

Question 3. Why was Kennedy murdered in public? President Kennedy was a sick man, taking a lot of pills daily. He had Addison's disease which, in addition to susceptibility to infection can cause weakness, weight loss and low blood pressure; so he was taking cortisone. For his back pain Dr. Max Jacobson injected him (and Jackie) with a mixture of unspecified (!) multivitamins, hormones, steroids, enzymes, and animal organ cells. Kennedy also used cocaine, marijuana, hashish and even LSD, especially during dates with women, including prostitutes — for many people this was not a secret. There were enough opportunities to stage a death in private.

Answer. This had to be a public execution with a very clear message for the next Presidents - "Don't touch the CIA!" and it worked until now. I want to touch CIA.

Question 4. What was the rush?
Answer. Kennedy wanted to eliminate CIA.
JFK's assassination was planned by a very professional expert. It might be Gestapo Mueller who, unlike other assassins, had a very good reason to keep his mouth shut. That's why Congress wants to keep 40,000 documents on JFK case classified for another 20 years.

June 5, 1968

Robert Kennedy shot

After winning the California primary election for the Democratic nomination for the US President, Senator Robert Kennedy was shot as he walked through the kitchen of the Ambassador Hotel. Sirhan Sirhan, a 24-year-old Palestinian immigrant, was convicted of Kennedy's murder and is serving a life sentence for the crime. Robert Kennedy promised a full investigation of his brother's assassination in case he was elected.

1995

John Kennedy and Diana

John Kennedy Jr. who said once that his father's death investigation was the most important thing of his life, approached Princess Diana Spencer for an interview for his "George" magazine. They met at New York Carlyle Hotel where JFK dated Marilyn Monroe - a holy place for John Kennedy Jr. where he would never have "hot sex" and "try cocaine" with Diana . It was a business meeting, an "investigation" meeting. In 1995 CIA wanted me to kill somebody very important - it could be Diana and John Kennedy Jr.

August 31, 1997
CIA used my instructions on staged car accidents to kill Princess Diana. Diana was fatally injured in a car crash in the Pont de l'Alma road tunnel in Paris, which also caused the death of her boyfriend, Dodi Fayed.

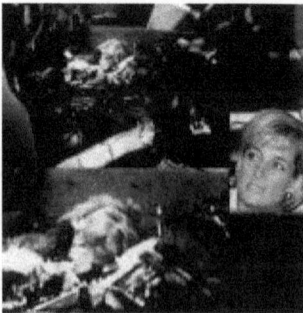

Diana is dead

Tenet, CIA Director (1997-2004)

Billionaire Mohammed al-Fayed, Dodi's father, recruited a "mole" inside CIA, somebody who knew the Agency had a file on Diana. He didn't get it of course through Washington, DC District Court and the mistake was - he had to recruit somebody with straight access to archives. If Diana left a notice on her talks with John Kennedy Jr for her sons, they might be next CIA victims. I can tell Mohammed al-Fayed what's in Diana's CIA file for free - surveillance documents, a video tape of the Carlyle Hotel meeting, a plan to stage the car accident, a file on me if I had to do the job.

If I have to investigate Diana's death, I would start with a very simple question: what happened to the driver, the Ritz security chief Henri Paul? He tried to out-run paparazzi by speeding down a Riverfront Expressway, but lost somehow control of the Mercedes S280 near the entrance to the Alma Tunnel and crashed into a concrete pillar at an estimated speed of 65 to 70 miles per hour. He died on impact of a severed spine and a ruptured aorta.

Attention. The tests showed an extraordinary high (not explained until now) level of carbon monoxide in his blood (20.7 %), which should have caused a severe headache, dizziness, confusion and absolute aversion to alcohol. Very heavy smokers can have a level of up to 9%, and Henri Paul was not a heavy smoker. There were no ventilation problems in his apartment, office or car. The gas didn't appear from inside Mercedes because no other passenger was affected. So, what happened to Henri Paul?

July 16, 1999
CIA killed John Kennedy Jr. in a staged plane crash. Kennedy along with his wife Carolyn and sister-in-law Lauren were reported missing when the Piper Saratoga II HP he was piloting failed to arrive at its planned destination, the Martha's Vineyard Airport in Vineyard Haven, Massachusetts.

John and wife Carolyn

A search immediately commenced to locate the trio, ending on July 21 when their bodies were discovered and returned to land. The National Transportation Safety Board (NTSB) determined that the plane had crashed into the Atlantic Ocean off Martha's Vineyard and the probable cause was pilot error: "Kennedy's failure to maintain control of the airplane during a descent over water at night, which was a result of spatial disorientation." Kennedy was not qualified to fly a plane by "instruments only," though the crash occurred in conditions not legally requiring it. Their ashes were scattered from the Navy ship off the coast of Martha's Vineyard.

CHAPTER 3
KGB Bill Clinton

December 31, 1969

Yuri Andropov, KGB Chief
1967-1982

Oxford student and anti-war activist Bill Clinton came to Moscow through Holland, Denmark, Norway, Sweden, and Finland for 5-days vacation at expensive "National" Hotel. The only person he knew in Moscow was Anik "Nikki" Alexis, a daughter of a French diplomat. Clinton recalls, "One night I took a bus out to Lumumba University to have dinner with Nikki". On the bus back home, Clinton says, there was only one other passenger, Oleg Rakito, who "spoke better English than I did" and "asked me lots of questions and told me he worked for the government, virtually admitting he was assigned to keep an eye on me".

The story is all fake. First, foreigners who can afford "National" don't use public transportation on January -30 C night. Second, KGB officer might reveal his identity to a foreigner if he's recruiting him only. Third, Bill Clinton was recruited; otherwise he would have left Moscow immediately and in panic. Instead, he enjoyed the rest of his vacation and went to Czechoslovakia, another socialist country. In 1969 Bill Clinton was 23, perfect age – KGB tried to recruit young foreigners (students of Yale, Harvard, Columbia, Oxford) between ages 21-26 because:

 a) you brainwash them much easier and faster than adults
 b) you build their careers the way you want

 Bill Clinton shared the story with Hillary, of course. KGB, not Hillary Clinton, made Bill Clinton Arkansas Governor and then – US President. Clinton was and is scared to death that sooner or later some "mole" inside Russian intelligence might point finger at him.

And that's how the report on his recruitment might look like.

Top secret

General of the Army Andropov Y.V
KGB Chairman
January 5, 1969

REPORT
On William Clinton recruitment

On January 4, 1969 Deputy Chief of the 1st Department of the KGB First Chief Directorate Colonel Smirnov A.V. recruited at the "National" Hotel

William Jefferson Clinton, born August 19, 1946 in Hope, Arkansas, USA, American citizen, single, the student of University College, Oxford, UK (Philosophy, Politics and Economics).

Our sources in Oxford, "Alice" and "Peter", characterize W. Clinton as a student with socialist views. He also participated in Vietnam War protests and organized an October 1969 Moratorium to End the War in Vietnam demonstration outside the US Embassy in London.

At the beginning of the meeting Smirnov discussed with the William Clinton the peaceful policy of the USSR Communist Party, the differences between capitalist and socialist systems, the benefits of social equality in our country. Clinton demonstrated deep understanding of the social problems in USA, advantages of socialism and importance to put an end to war in Vietnam. He also admitted that Russians are very open and honest people.

Colonel Smirnov explained to Clinton that Soviet leadership is planning to improve relations with the United States and it depends not only on the US President Richard Nixon and the General Secretary of the USSR Communist party, but also on activity of young people, students like Clinton. That's why KGB is asking him to be a part of this process which is of vital importance for Soviet and American people. In the future KGB can help him in his political career. Secret cooperation will be rewarded ($500 a month).

William Clinton gave his consent and signed a statement about cooperation with KGB. He said that since he met President John Kennedy on July 24, 1963 while attending the Boys Nation he's dreaming about presidency.

In the future we plan to help Bill Clinton to get to the top positions in American politics and start the process in his native Arkansas state.

Chief of the KGB First Chief Directorate
Lieutenant General A.M. Sakharovsky

July 20, 1993
Bill Clinton tried to move America towards socialism through health care reform plan. His effort ultimately died, though Obama finished the job.

1997
Much more important – Russia, totalitarian, 100% corrupted country with dying economy and dictator Boris Yeltsin ("Czar Boris") on top, joined the G7, a group of seven major industrialized democracies (USA, Canada, Great Britain, France, Italy, Germany, Japan). It was all KGB source Bill Clinton's huge effort which had no explanation at all - now you have it.

How and how much Russians paid Bill Clinton?

In 1993 Vice President Gore and Russian Prime Minister Chernomyrdin signed a 20-year $12 billion deal under which Russia would ship its weapons-grade uranium to the United States.

Bill Clinton in his over 1,000-page memoir My Life (2004) wrote actually nothing about this "deal of a century." Look,

"In the afternoon [April, 3, 1993] we [Clinton and Russian President Yeltsin] agreed on a way to institutionalize cooperation, with a commission headed by Vice President Gore and Russian Prime Minister Victor Chernomyrdin.

Clinton and Yeltsin

The idea was developed by Strobe [Talbott] and Georgi Mamedov, the Russian Deputy Foreign Minister, and it worked better than any of us could have imagined, thanks largely to the consistent and concentrated efforts made over the years by Al Gore and his Russian counterparts in working through a host of difficult, contentious problems" [p. 507].

"On January 30 [1996], Prime Minister Victor Chernomyrdin of Russia came to the White House for his sixth meeting with Al Gore. After they finished their commission business, Chernomyrdin came to see me to brief me on events in Russia and Yeltsin's prospects for reelection" [p. 697].

That's it.

Questions

What idea was "developed" by Talbot?

What extremely secret commission was "headed by Gore and Chernomyrdin"?

Why Clinton was so happy that "it worked better than any of us could have imagined"?

What "commission business" did Al Gore and his partner finish on January 30, 1996?

Answers

At their summit meeting in Vancouver, in April 1993, President Clinton and President Yeltsin created the U.S.–Russian Joint Commission on Economic and Technological Cooperation. Since then it has become known as the Gore–Chernomyrdin Commission (GCC), after its co-chairmen US Vice President Al Gore and Russian Prime Minister Victor Chernomyrdin. The Commission's original mandate was to support cooperation between the United States and Russia in the areas of space, energy and high technology.

In fact it was a ruse to mask work on a non-proliferation agreement to convert highly enriched uranium (HEU) taken from dismantled Russian nuclear warheads into low-enriched uranium (LEU) fuel to be sold to customers in the USA and worldwide through the USEC (United States Enrichment Company). USEC was created in 1993 as a government corporation with the mission to restructure the US government's uranium enrichment operation and to prepare it for sale to the private sector.

Attention. On April 26, 1996 Bill Clinton signed into law the USEC Privatization Act. The HEU Agreement required the United States to purchase through USEC 500 metric tons, $12 billion worth, of HEU.

Dead Russians: Three Russian statesmen tried to investigate the Clinton- Yeltsin deal - Ruvim Nureyev, Lev Rokhlin, Yuri Shchekotchikhin. All of them are dead.

1. Ruvim Nureyev. The Russia Chief Inspector for Nuclear and Radiation Safety, who strongly opposed the deal, was found dead

on the railroad tracks in June 1996. The incident was described as a suicide.

2. Lev Rokhlin. The Russian State Duma Deputy Lieutenant General Lev Rokhlin was a politician of rare honesty and bravity. In 1998 Rokhlin started his own official Clinton-Yeltsin deal investigation. Lev Maximov, the Nuclear Technologies Institute Director, who helped Rokhlin to obtain the documents, received death threats.

General Lev Roklhin

On July 3, 1998 Rokhlin was shot three times and killed in his house while he was sleeping. His wife, Tamara Rokhlina, was arrested and testified that she killed him "for reasons of personal enmity." She later recanted her testimony, saying she incriminated herself under threat. Rokhlin's bodyguard, who was there that night, testified that he heard no gunshots (the killers used a silencer). Within days three more dead bodies were found in the vicinity of the Rokhlin household and were cremated before they could be identified. In November 2000, Rokhlina was convicted of murder and sentenced to 8 years in prison, but the Supreme Court overturned the verdict and ordered a new trial.

On October 2, 1998 the US Congress, taking into account that Lev Rokhlin was a former Russian State Duma Defense Committee Chairman, asked President Clinton to "urge the Russia Government to promptly and thoroughly investigate" the case. Of course, Bill Clinton was smart enough not to dig his own grave, and just ignored this

RESOLUTION

Expressing sympathy to the family and collegues of Lev Yakovlevich Rokhlin, and expressing the sense of the House of Representatives that President of the United States should urge the Russia Government to promptly and thoroughly investigate the circumstances surrounding the death of Lev Yakovlevich Rokhlin and to provide a full accounting of the circumstances as soon as practible, but no later than November 1999.

Whereas Lev Rokhlin assumed the chairmanship of the Defense Committee of the Duma and was the highest-ranking elected official in the Duma working on Defense issues...

Whereas Lev Rokhlin became involved in investigation of illegal arms from Russia to Armenia and other nations.

Whereas in October 1997, Lev Rokhlin advocated the resignation of President Yeltsyn.

Whereas attempts were made for 6 months to remove Lev Rokhlin from his Committee chairmanship.

Whereas on July 3, 1998, Lev Rokhlin was stripped of the chairmanship of the Defense Committee, but maintained his position as a member of Duma.

Whereas on July 3, 1998, Lev Rokhlin was shot in the head three times and killed.

Whereas members of Lev Rokhlin's family have stated that Rokhlin's wife, Tamara Pavlovna Rokhlina, was physically abused and was threatened with death unless she accepted responsibility for Lev Rokhlin's murder.

Whereas Lev Rokhlin's bodyguard, who was in the home the night of the murder, claimed that he heard no gunshots.

Whereas three bodies were cremated by the Moscow government authorities before they could be identified.

Whereas any inability of Russia to provide a full accounting of the circumstances surrounding the death of Lev Rokhlin would raise serious questions about the existence of a stable democratic system in Russia:

Now, therefore, be it resolved, that –
(1) The House of Representatives expresses sympathy to the family and colleagues of Lev Rokhlin and:

(2) It is the sense of the House of Representatives that the President of the United States should urge the Russian Government –
(a) to promptly and thoroughly investigate the circumstances surrounding the death of Lev Rokhlin;
(b) to provide a full accounting of circumstances as soon as practicable, but not later than November,1999

3. Yuri Shchekotchikhin, a famous Russian reporter and corruption fighter, was elected to the Russian State Duma where he served as National Security Committee Deputy.

Yuri Shchekotchikhin

After Rokhlin was murdered in 1998, Shchekotchikhin continued his investigation and concentrated his efforts in two directions: first, he tried to obtain the #1 Gore–Chernomyrdin Agreement (September 2, 1993), but President Yeltsin and then President Putin denied the requests. Second, he started a full-scale investigation into the Atomic Ministry corruption and — against Atomic Minister Adamov in person (again, see file 4). On June 16, 2003, he lost consciousness and was taken to the Central (Kremlin) Hospital. He was pronounced dead after lying still unconscious for 12 days. (The official diagnosis - a flu). All medical records are still classified, but experts insist he was poisoned by thallium or cadmium.

Top secret thief Adamov and Clintons
Professor Adamov was in 1986-1998 a Director of the NIKIET (a secret Research and Development Institute of Power Engineering).

Eugene Adamov   **Lanny Breuer**

He was secretly involved in the Gore–Chernomyrdin deal as chief expert on the Russian side (even Russian Defense Minister Rodionov knew nothing about it). In 1994 he opened the consulting and management company "Omeka, Ltd." registered in Pennsylvania (by the end of 1999 the company had assets valued of $5,080,000) by his wife. In 1996 he signed a forged contract between NIKIET and "Omeka," and opened other companies and banking accounts in Monaco, Switzerland and France to start money laundering the stolen funds the US Department of Energy provided Russia to improve safety at Russian nuclear facilities.

On May 2, 2005 Adamov was arrested in Bern, Switzerland, and was charged with conspiracy to defraud the United States and to transfer stolen money and securities ($9 million), money laundering and tax evasion. US prosecutors demanded his extradition to the United States, but Russia did the same, asking to send Adamov back home where he would be faced a trial. Swiss authorities asked Adamov if he was willing to accept simplified extradition to the United States. He rejected that and Washington had to file a formal extradition request. The battle began.

A money laundering blew up into an international scandal. The American government's insistence looked strange until Bill Clinton appeared on the stage on October 5, 2005 to save Adamov from 60 years in jail. He didn't show up himself. Somebody hired a lawyer - Lanny Breuer, a nice young fellow from the Washington, DC based "Covington & Burling." Breuer had worked as a special Counsel to President Clinton in 1997-

1999 and represented him in the presidential impeachment hearings and trial.

This was not a battle between Russia and USA - it was a battle between the Republicans and Democrats for the Oval Office in 2008. Russians and their asset Bill Clinton had to win this struggle no matter what — if Adamov was extradited to America, he would "sing" everything on that Clinton-Yeltsin deal and share his federal cell with Bill Clinton.

Meanwhile President Bush, a Republican, needed victory to remove the Clintons from the political arena forever. Clinton won - on December 18, 2005 the Swiss Supreme Court overturned a previous ruling by the Justice Ministry, which had said that Adamov must first face the US courts. On December 30, 2005 Adamov was extradited from Switzerland to Russia, thus opening the door to the Big Presidential Game for Hillary Clinton. She lost in 2008. What price will the Russians ask Hillary Clinton to pay for Adamov's silence, if she's elected the US President in 2016?

How much Russians paid to Bill Clinton after the 1993 "deal" was signed?

CHAPTER 4
"Kremlin"

September 1991- June 1992

My KGB intelligence officer career came to an end when USSR collapsed in 1991. Next 2 years, as SBU (Ukrainian Security) illegal spy under cover of political analyst, I worked in Moscow (operation "Kremlin"). My job was to get into Russian President Boris Yeltsin "inner circle" and influence his decisions, extremely anti-Ukrainian at the time. I met people who knew Yeltsin well, like Russian Parliament Constitutional Committee Chairman Rumyantsev and one of Yeltsin's photographers, who asked me to work for him.

In February 1992, I could kill Yeltsin if ordered so by Ukrainian President Kravchuk.

L. Kravchuk
President of Ukraine

B. Yeltsin (l.) and his successor
V. Putin

As a former KGB "Nabat" (anti-terror) group sniper I knew perfectly well how they protected Yeltsin. Besides, in 1986 I joined A. Gromyko, Chairman of the USSR Supreme Soviet (actually, the USSR President), security team during his visit to Gorky city and it was a big experience too. I was working alone, though you have to send three groups for operation like this one : surveillance (with optics and radios), action (includes snipers, explosives technicians or staged accidents specialists), and security (these people neutralize bodyguards, witnesses and other people who could interrupt the action; they complete the action if the action group fails; and they can neutralize the action group later, if planned so; they "cover" the safe retreat of action group and "cut" the chase.

Operation was in progress until there was a leak and Yeltsin got information about it. In 1992 Russia and Ukraine signed a Treaty to stop mutual espionage. President Kravchuk ordered to kill me as a witness of his dirty politics. I moved to Poland and then, in 1995, to USA.

CIA decided to copy "Kremlin" in Washington, DC and that brings to the scene.

CHAPTER 5
Meet KGB "Mole" Deutch, CIA Director

John Deutch

Deutch was born in Belgium to a Russian father and he was the only Russian CIA Director. He got some jobs with top secrets access positions:

1977-1980 The US Department of Energy: Director of Energy Research, Acting Assistant Secretary for Energy Technology, Under Secretary
1980-1981 President's Nuclear Safety Oversight Commission
1983 President's Commission on Strategic Forces
1985-1989 The White House Science Council
1990-1993 The President's Intelligence Advisory Board
1993-1994 Under Secretary of Defense for Acquisition and Technology, Deputy Defense Secretary
1995-1996 Director of Central Intelligence
1996 The President's Commission on Aviation Safety and Security
1998-1999 Chairman of the Commission to Assess the Organization of the Federal Government to Combat the Proliferation of Weapons of Mass Destruction
He was appointed by President Clinton and stayed in Langley in 1995-1996. He ordered my recruitment, he is a Russian "mole," and he's safe because Bill Clinton pardoned this enemy of state in 2001.

Three signs are enough to triangulate a "mole" and here they are for Mr. Deutch:

1. Two days after Deutch retired from the CIA, on December 16, 1996, technical personnel discovered at his house highly classified information stored on his unclassified computer, loaded from his agency computer. He refused to explain why he violated strict security rules.

First, Director of Central Intelligence doesn't need highly classified data on his home computer, because he is a bureaucrat, not an analyst.

Second, here we have a trick - the Internet-connected computer is accessible by anyone with some technical knowledge and you don't have to send anything — Russians will read secret information right from your home computer.

2. In 1997 the CIA began a formal security investigation. It was determined that his computer was often connected to Internet with no security, and that Deutch was known to leave memory cards with classified data lying in his car. Deutch used his influence to stop further investigation and the CIA took no action until 1999, when it suspended his security clearances. He admitted finally the security breach and merely apologized but refused to explain communication via Internet with some Russian chemist.

3. In 1999 the Defense Department started its own investigation, and it appeared that in 1993 Deutch, as Defense Undersecretary, used unsecured computers at home and his America Online (!) account to access classified defense information. As Deputy Defense Secretary, he declined departmental requests in 1994 to allow security systems to be installed in his residence.

In 2000 Senator Charles Grassley asked the Justice Department to look into the case. There was no investigation. In 2001 President Clinton pardoned Deutch. There were no comments.

Hillary Clinton wrote in her book *Living History: "Jackie* [Kennedy - M.K.]... She never came out and said it, but she meant that he [Bill Clinton - M.K] might also be a target. 'He has to be very careful," she told me. "Very careful" In 1991, dying from lung cancer, Jackie Kennedy was still scared to talk about CIA.

Since 2000 Deutch is MIT Professor and Director for Citigroup. Very good.

CHAPTER 6
"Millennium Hilton" Grand Conspiracy

September 1, 1995

I was recruited at "Millennium Hilton", NYC as CIA "Filament" by CIA agents Bill and Joe .I also met Frank from FBI National Security Division and had to work for two agencies.

Next was a joint CIA-FBI conspiracy. They decided to "copy" "Kremlin" operation I had to spy on the U.S. Congress and work with Congress Librarian James Billington who knew me as a political scientist through his Moscow office, and could introduce to Senators and Representatives.

I had to influence the White House and create "The Professional" system - special instructions for Bill Clinton on successful election and re-election campaigns, strategic planning and top decisions making, national security, foreign policy and diplomacy, propaganda, economy, war and special operations.

Since 2009 Obama is using "The Professional" too (see "Bonus").

Like James Bond in Hollywood movies, I had a unique CIA status, "carte blanche" ("stay in USA as long as you want and do whatever you think is necessary" which means also a "license to kill") and understood that control over the White House and the U.S. Congress, not national security, was the CIA/FBI top priority.

Besides, they were interested in effective interrogation, tortures and murders methods – I gave them instructions and that was a big help in Guantanamo, Iraq and Afghanistan. I visited Washington, DC, met people there and estimated the White House and U.S. Congress security.

CIA also had "a very important job up to my "high professional skills as a sniper" but I didn't want to kill politicians and become Lee Oswald #2. They've pressed me very hard in return.

Date: ~~JUL 2 5 1997~~

Mr. Mykhaylo Ivanovich Kryzhanovsky
3801 18th Ave. Apt 1-H
Brooklyn, NY 11218

File: A73 670 254

Asylum Approval

Dear Mr. Kryzhanovsky:

This letter refers to your request for asylum in the United States filed on Form I-589. This office previously issued you a letter to notify you that your request for asylum had been recommended for approval, pending the results of the mandatory, confidential investigation of your identity and background.

It has been determined that you are eligible for asylum in the United States. Attached please find a completed Form I-94, Arrival Departure Record, indicating that you have been granted asylum status in the United States pursuant to §208(a) of the Immigration and Nationality Act (INA) as of JUL 2 5 1997. You have been granted asylum in the United States for an indefinite period. This grant of asylum includes your dependents listed above who are present in the United States, were included in your asylum application, and for whom you have established a qualifying relationship by a preponderance of evidence.

In order to request derivative asylum status for any spouse or child who was not included in your asylum request, you must submit a Form I-730, Refugee and Asylee Relative Petition, to the Immigration and Naturalization Service (INS).

You are eligible for employment authorization for as long as you remain in asylum status. Your dependents listed above are also eligible for employment authorization, so long as they retain derivative asylum status. However, you must apply for and obtain an Employment Authorization Document (EAD) as evidence of your eligibility to work in the United States. To obtain an EAD, you must submit to the INS a Form I-765, Application for Employment Authorization. We suggest that you include a copy of this letter when applying for work authorization as an asylee.

If you plan to depart the United States, you must obtain permission to return to the United States before you leave this country. If you do not obtain permission, you may be unable to reenter the United States, or you may be placed in proceedings where you will be required to establish your asylum status. You may apply for a Refugee Travel Document on a Form I-131, Application for Travel Document.

Asylum status does not give you the right to remain permanently in the United States. Asylum status may be terminated if you no longer have a well-founded fear of persecution because of a fundamental change in circumstances, you have obtained protection from another country, or you

CIA rules the government: I got immigration status in 5 minutes.

Bill Clinton was the target because CIA wanted me "to stay close to him" - that's why I wrote a handbook for him. It's interesting that in 1995 he started dating Monica Lewinsky in the White House and his wife, Hillary Clinton, was there on two occasions, at least. She knew about the dates, she overreacted and asked CIA Director John Deutch for a "favor". I've refused to do "a big job" and Bill Clinton has to say "Thank you very much, Mike, for saving my life". In 2001, Bill pardoned John Deutch whom he completely ignored before because Hillary Clinton asked him to do so. She was scared Deutch might talk about a "favor" in case there was some serious investigation about his "security problems".

There might be one more reason to eliminate Clinton – he didn't share "uranium" money he got from Russians with CIA.

"Filomena "restaurant, Washington, D.C., Bill Clinton's favorite. All you need to eliminate the guy is a decent sniper rifle, like M21 which you can use from a distance of 690m with effective accuracy.

In 2001 I asked Senator Hillary Clinton to help me fight CIA which kept pressing me - I couldn't get my family here. I asked Lus Mendes, Hillary Clinton's Immigration Department Chief to tell her boss that I've saved Bill Clinton's life by refusing to work for CIA. After that Hillary Clinton wrote to me 2 letters promising help - and she did help. She had no choice because it was a blackmail, KGB style, sorry.

June 21, 2001

Three months before 9/11 tragedy happened, I warned President George W. Bush, the House, the US Senate, including Senator Hillary Clinton, on CIA anti-American activity, national security collapse and my personal situation.

Hillary Clinton, the U.S. Senator in 2001-2009

Hillary Clinton refused to mess with CIA. I had to blackmail her and remind her that I helped Bill Clinton to win re-elections and saved his life. Hillary was scared to death and answered me in a year - finally, she helped my family only. Later she said: "KGB agent has no soul" - you may think it was about Russian leader Putin, but it was actually about me.

Now Hillary Clinton has to take some responsibility for the deaths of 3,000 innocent victims - why not?

HILLARY RODHAM CLINTON
NEW YORK
SENATOR

RUSSELL SENATE OFFICE BUILDING
SUITE 476
WASHINGTON, DC 20510-3204
202-224-4451

United States Senate

WASHINGTON, DC 20510-3204

August 23, 2001

Mr. Mykhaylo Kryzhanovsky
261 Lenox Road, Apt 4P
Brooklyn, New York 11226

Dear Mr. Kryzhanovsky:

Thank you for contacting my office for assistance. The trust and confidence that your request for assistance represents is very important to me. A Constituent Liaison has been assigned to handle your matter and you should be hearing from my office very soon.

Sincerely yours,

Hillary Rodham Clinton

Hillary Rodham Clinton

HRC/jlk

48

HILLARY RODHAM CLINTON
NEW YORK
SENATOR

United States Senate

WASHINGTON, DC 20510–3204

September 12, 2002

Mr. Mykhaylo Kryzhanovsky
20 Crooke Avenue Apt 6C
Brooklyn, New York 11226

Dear Mr. Kryzhanovsky:

Thank you for contacting my office for assistance with your matter. I have contacted the Immigration and Naturalization Service at the Nebraska Service Center on your behalf – attached is the response to my inquiry. I hope this information will be of help to you.

If I can be of further assistance to you, please do not hesitate to contact my office again.

Sincerely yours,

Hillary Rodham Clinton

Hillary Rodham Clinton

HRC/lm

106906

Why President Bush supported me?

President Bush and Obama

September 17, 2002

White House sent a request to the Dept. of Justice, where FBI Director Robert Mueller blocked it because I was a "joint" CIA-FBI project.

THE WHITE HOUSE

WASHINGTON

September 17, 2002

Dear Mr. Kryzhanovsky:

Thank you for contacting President George W. Bush for assistance with an agency of the Federal government. I am responding on behalf of the President.

The White House is sending your inquiry to the Department of Justice, which will review your correspondence. This agency has the expertise to address your concerns. They will respond directly to you, as promptly as possible.

The President sends his best wishes.

Sincerely,

Desiree Thompson
Special Assistant to the President
and Director of Presidential Correspondence

Republican National Committee Platinum Card

In 2006 Republican National Committee sent me a platinum member card with a very interesting letter saying I'm one of the leaders President Bush can trust. It was a sign President Bush supported my war against CIA.

319 First Street, SE,
Washington, DC 20003
May 20, 2006
PLATINUM MEMBER

Mykhaylo Kryzhanovsky
Member since 2006

This Platinum card has been issued to the bearer by the Republican national Committee in recognition of an extraordinary level of commitment to Republican ideals and values.

The bearer of this card should be given special considerations by all Republican leaders as one who has provided the lifeblood of our Party over many years.

I believe your exemplary record of loyalty and patriotism proves you are a leader President Bush can count on. It is therefore my distinct privilege as the Chairman of the Republican National Committee (RNC) to present you with your 2006 Republican Party Platinum Card on behalf of President Bush and every Republican leader nationwide.

Your leadership as one of our Party's elite Platinum Card holders is critical to electing principled Republicans in this year crucial midterm elections and implementing P{resident Bush's agenda.

President Bush is counting on proud Americans like you to stand with him this year - and to help him make sure the policies we support and the Republican candidates who share your values do not fall to defeat by the forces of partisan politics.

I believe your exemplary record of loyalty and patriotism proves you are a leader President Bush can trust to fight with him for America's safety and security. Your proven leadership is just what President Bush and our party need right now.

Please accept this honor with my sincere thanks.

Sincerely,
Ken Mehlman,
Chairman, Republican National Committee

Schumer's "Leadership"
September 20, 2008

Who else could help me to stop the CIA conspiracy? Of course, my senator, Chuck Schumer, a Democrat, who represents the New York State. I've contacted his office and we had a very long talk with the Office Director Suzan Orloff, who explained to me that **"American national security is not Senator's business"**. Senator Schumer is too busy to see me. And you call this the U.S. Senate leadership? I call this stupidity.

Schumer was chairman of the Democratic Senatorial Campaign Committee from 2005 to 2009. **He is the third-ranking Democrat in the Senate**, behind Senate Majority Leader Harry Reid and Senate Majority Whip Dick Durbin, elected Vice Chairman of the Democratic Caucus in the Senate in 2006. In November 2010, he was also chosen to hold the additional role of chairman of the Senate Democratic Policy Committee.

So, this guy is one of the U.S. Senate leaders and it's nice that our national security, security of our families, and our kids is "not his business". And you know what? He's dreaming about presidency. No way, Schumer!

June 8, 2010

U.S. OFFICE OF SPECIAL COUNSEL
1730 M Street, N.W., Suite 218
Washington, D.C. 20036-4505
202-254-3600

June 8, 2010

Mr. Mikhail Kryzhanovsky

VIA E-MAIL (prof7prof@yahoo.com)

Re: OSC File No: HA-10-2641

Dear Mr. Kryzhanovsky:

This letter is in response to the complaint you filed with the Office of Special Counsel (OSC) regarding the Hatch Act. Specifically, you allege that Mr. Leon Panetta violated the Hatch Act through his role in the "Millennium Hilton" operation. We reviewed this matter, and as explained below, we are closing our file without further action.

The Hatch Act (5 U.S.C. §§ 7321-7326) governs the political activity of most federal executive branch employees. The Act permits most employees to actively participate in partisan political management and partisan political campaigns. Employees, however, are prohibited from: using their official authority or influence for the purpose of affecting the result of an election; knowingly soliciting, accepting or receiving political contributions from any person; being candidates for public office in partisan elections; and knowingly soliciting or discouraging the political activity of any individual with business before their agency. 5 U.S.C. § 7323(a)(1)-(4). The Hatch Act also prohibits employees from engaging in political activity while on duty, in a government building, while wearing an official uniform or insignia or in an official vehicle. 5 U.S.C. § 7324.

Your allegation that Mr. Panetta is involved in a CIA-FBI conspiracy, which you call the "Millennium Hilton" operation, even if true, is not activity that falls within the prohibitions of the Hatch Act. Therefore, we are closing the above referenced file.

Sincerely,

Erica S. Hamrick
Deputy Chief
Hatch Act Unit

53

US Office of Special Counsel Patrick Fitzgerald (his predecessor, Ken Starr, brought Bill Clinton to impeachment):
"Mr. Kryzhanovsky, You allege that Mr. Leon Panetta violated the Hatch Act through his role in the "Millennium Hilton" operation. We reviewed this matter, and as explained below, we are closing our file without further action. The Hatch Act prohibits government employees from engaging in political activity while on duty. *__Your allegation that Mr. Panetta is involved in a CIA-FBI conspiracy, which you call the "Millennium Hilton" operation, even if true,__* is not activity that falls within the prohibitions of the Hatch Act. Therefore, we are closing the above referenced file. Erica S. Hamrick"

Patrick Fitzgerald

February 6, 2011
"Mr. Kryzhanovsky: The New York City Commission on Human Rights does not have jurisdiction over the agencies you take issue with. Talk to Attorney General, the CIA, The US Congress. Cliff Mulqueen, Deputy Commissioner/General Counsel, New York City Commission on Human Rights".

President Obama and Janet Napolitano, Homeland Security Secretary keep silence. What's going on now? CIA is pressing me non-stop, so the following CIA Directors were involved in the conspiracy: John Deutch (1995-1996), George Tenet (1997-2004), Porter Goss (2004-2006), Gen. Michael Hayden (2006-2009), Leon Panetta (2009-2011), Gen. David Petraeus.

June 21, 2001, 81 days before 9/11 tragedy
I've sent a letter to the following US Senators on America's national security collapse and CIA anti-American activity:

Richard Shelby, Jeff Sessions (R), Ted Stevens (R), Frank Murkowski (R), Lisa Murkowski (R), John McCain (R), 2008 presidential election candidate, Jon Kyl (R), Tim Hutchinson (R), Blanche Lincoln (D), Dianne Feinstein (D), Barbara Boxer (D), Ben Campbell (R), Wayne Allard (R), Christopher Dodd (D), Joseph Lieberman (D), Joe Biden (D), the US Vice President since 2009, Tom Carper (D), Bob Graham (D), Bill Nelson (D), Max Cleland (D), Zell Miller (D),Daniel Inouye (D), Daniel Akaka (D), Larry Craig (R), Mike Crapo (R), Richard Durbin (D), Peter Fitzgerald (R), Richard Lugar (R), Evan Bayh (D), Chuck Grassley, Tom Harkin (D), Sam Brownback (R), Pat Roberts (R), Mitch McConnell (R), Jim Bunning (R), John Breaux (D), Mary Landrieu (D), Olympia Snowe (R), Susan Collins (R), Paul Sarbanes (D), Barbara Mikulski (D), Ted Kennedy (D), John Kerry (D), 2004 presidential election candidate, Carl Levin (D), Debbie Stabenow (D), Paul Wellstone (D), Mark Dayton (D), Thad Cochran (R), Trent Lott (R), Kit Bond (R), Jean Carnahan (D), Max Baucus (D), Conrad Burns (R), Chuck Hagel (R), Ben Nelson (D), Harry Reid (D),John Ensign (R), Bob Smith (R),Judd Gregg (R), Robert Torricelli (D), Jon Corzine (D), Pete Domenici (R), Jeff Bingaman (D), Charles Schumer (D), Hillary Clinton (D), US Secretary of State since 2009, Jesse Helms (R), John Edwards (D), Kent Conrad (D), Byron Dorgan (D), Mike DeWine (R), George Voinovich (R), Don Nickles (R), James Inhofe (R), Ron Wyden (D), Gordon Smith (R), Arlen Specter (R), Rick Santorum (R), Jack Reed (D), Lincoln Chafee (R), Strom Thurmond (R),Ernest Hollings (D), Tom Daschle (D), Tim Johnson (D), Fred Thompson (R), Bill Frist (R), Phil Gramm (R), Kay Bailey Hutchison (R), Orrin Hatch (R), Robert Bennett (R), Patrick Leahy (D), John Warner (R), George Allen (R), Patty Murray (D), Maria Cantwell (D),

Robert Byrd (D), Jay Rockefeller (D), Herbert Kohl (D), Russ Feingold (D), Craig Thomas (R),Michael Enzi (R)

Nobody wanted to get a bullet from CIA sniper, right Mr. Joe Biden? Senator Hillary Clinton was the only one who responded under pressure in August, 2011.

Forget it, Biden, I'm not joking.

Still in the office:
Daniel Akaka (D - HI), Max Baucus (D - MT), Jeff Bingaman(D - NM), Barbara Boxer (D - CA), Maria Cantwell, (D - WA), Thomas Carper, (D - DE), Thad Cochran, (R - MS), Susan Collins, (R - ME), Kent Conrad, (D - ND), Mike Crapo, (R - ID), Richard Durbin, (D - IL), Michael Enzi, (R - WY), Dianne Feinstein (D - CA),Chuck Grassley (R - IA), Tom Harkin (D - IA), Orrin Hatcch (R - UT), Kay Bailey Hutchison (R - TX), James Inhofe (R - OK), Daniel Inouye (D - HI), Tim Johnson (D - SD), John Kerry (D - MA), Herb Kohl,(D - WI), Jon Kyl, (R - AZ), Mary Landrieu (D - LA),Patrick Leahy (D - VT), Carl Levin (D - MI), Joseph Lieberman (ID - CT), Richard Lugar (R - IN), John McCain (R – AZ), Mitch McConnell (R - KY), Barbara Mikulski (D - MD), Patty Murray (D - WA),Ben Nelson (D - NE), Bill Nelson, (D - FL), Rand Paul (R - KY), Jack Reed (D - RI), Harry Reid (D - NV), Pat Roberts (R - KS), John Rockefeller (D - WV), Chuck Schumer (D - NY), Jeff Sessions (R - AL), Richard Shelby (R - AL),Olympia Snowe, (R - ME), Debbie Stabenow (D - MI), Ron Wyden (D - OR).

Nobody bothered. Not interested or interested a lot? If Joe Biden, a former Senator, wants to run for President in 2016, I wish him bad luck.

How I would plan special operation like this one?
I'm sure the CIA followed the same scheme (and used their own satellites for technical support).

1. Objectives.
al-Qaeda to be blamed, Iraq to be invaded, oil to be taken.

2. Preparation.
CIA undercover explained to Bin-Laden unusual plan to attack America. The plan approved, terrorists sent to USA.
Another group of terrorists, no links to al-Qaeda, was allowed to pack Twin Towers with explosives. Right after the #2 terrorist team was eliminated, their bodies burnt.

3. Action.
September 11, 2001
19 al-Qaeda terrorists boarded 4 jets.

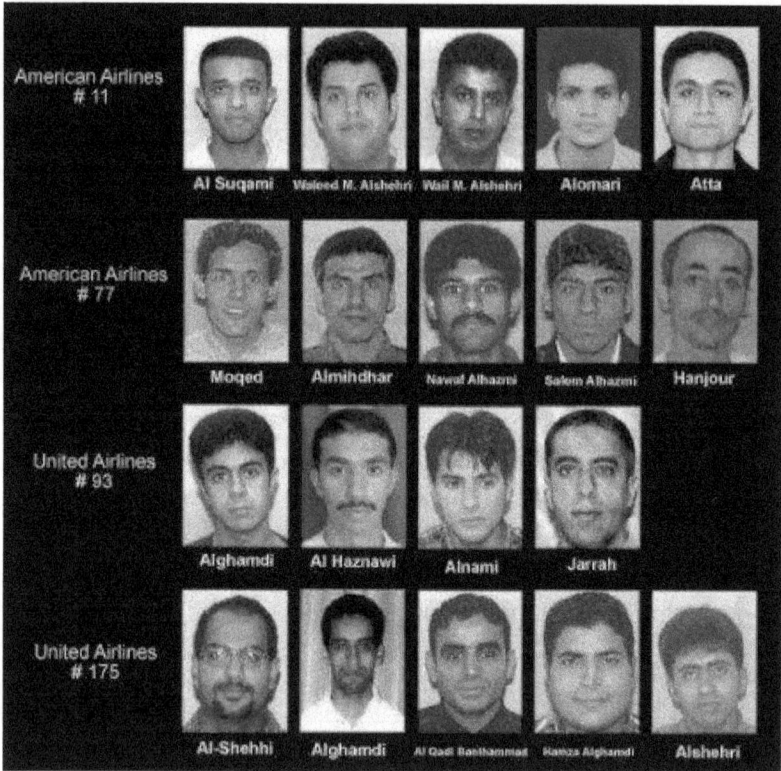

American Airlines #11: Al Suqami, Waleed M. Alshehri, Wail M. Alshehri, Alomari, Atta

American Airlines #77: Moqed, Almihdhar, Nawaf Alhazmi, Salem Alhazmi, Hanjour

United Airlines #93: Alghamdi, Al Haznawi, Alnami, Jarrah

United Airlines #175: Al-Shehhi, Alghamdi, Al Qadi Banihammad, Hamza Alghamdi, Alshehri

Right after that they were secretly arrested, taken away and killed. Their bodies burnt.

8 a.m. EDT. American airlines Flight 11, a Boeing 767 with 92 people on board, took off from Boston's Logan International Airport to Los Angeles.
8:14 a.m. United Airlines Flight 175, a Boeing 767 with 65 people on board, took off from Logan to Los Angeles.
8:21 a.m. American Airlines flight 77, a Boeing 757 with 64 people on board, took off from Washington Dulles International Airport for Los Angeles.
8:41 a.m. United Airlines Flight 93, a Boeing 757 with 44 people on board, took off from Newark International Airport for San Francisco.

After 4 jets took off, their pilots were ordered emergency landing on one of the military bases where crews and passengers boarded another jet packed with explosives. It exploded in the air and crashed into a field in Pennsylvania. Two other empty jets, guided by autopilots, with explosives crashed into Twin Towers.

Cruise missile hit Pentagon. I'll pay $1, 000, 000 to anybody who'll melt a piece of steel with kerosene jet-fuel.

Osama Bin-Laden was sure he did it.

After Bin-Laden's death al-Qaeda has to prove its strength one more time and attack two more American symbols - Capitol or the White House. Wait.

THE BIGGEST LIE ABOUT 9/11

I'll pay $1, 000, 000 to anybody who'll melt a piece of steel with kerosene jet-fuel.

Thank you, Edward Snowden
October 2, 2013

Thank you, Edward Snowden. I hope you'll tell also of how National Security Agency helped CIA, FBI and the U.S. Secret Service with surveillance on the White House and the U.S. Congress and murders on American territory - the operation I was involved since 1995.

Investigative reporter Jeremy Scahill told an audience in Brazil that he and Guardian journalist Glenn Greenwald are working on a project involving "how the National Security Agency plays a significant, central role in the U.S. assassination program." The information apparently comes from classified

NSA documents leaked by Edward Snowden. We know a bit about the NSA's connection to America's global capture/kill machine already.

In the 2010 report "Top secret America", Dana Priest and Will Arkin of *The Washington Post* reported that the NSA provided the capture/kill squads of Joint Special Operations Command (JSOC) with a huge advantage after the signals intelligence agency "learned to locate all electronic signals in Iraq."

In 2011 Spencer Ackerman of Wired reported that the NSA created a system called "the Real Time Regional Gateway" that allowed the sharing of intelligence from raids and interrogations across the JSOC network. JSOC worked closely with two intelligence units that would help provide JSOC with real-time intelligence to "fuel a global manhunt".

The Army's Intelligence Support Activity (i.e., the "Activity"), JSOC's in-house intelligence wing, specialized in operational electronic surveillance and intercepts.

In 2002 Defense Secretary Donald Rumsfeld established the Strategic Support Branch (SSB), which included "new clandestine teams" made up of "case officers, linguists, interrogators and technical specialists" who were deployed alongside JSOC forces. Together these teams contributed to a system where JSOC's intelligence operations "were feeding its action and often that intelligence was not vetted by anyone outside of the JSOC structure," Scahill writes. "The priority was to keep hitting targets". The insulated intelligence led to a lot of people being killed - some of whom were innocent.

"You go in and you get some intelligence... and [7th special forces group, Department of Defense] kill 27, 30, 40 people, whatever, and they capture seven or eight," U.S. Army Colonel Lawrence Wilkerson (Ret.), who served as Secretary of State Colin Powell's chief of staff (2002-05), told Scahill. "Then you find out that the intelligence was bad and you killed a bunch of innocent people and you have a bunch of innocent people on your hands, so you stuff 'em in Guantanamo. No one ever knows anything about that".

PART 2

KGB OPERATION "BARACK OBAMA"

CHAPTER 1
"Obama", KGB Illegal Spy

Pic 1   Pic 2

Pic 1. Barack Obama in 1971, age 10 and how he might look in 2001, age 40 - face aged on *in20years.com*
Pic 2. Barack Obama in 2000, official photo.
Any difference?

August 4, 1961
Barack Obama was born in Honolulu, Hawaii.
If there's something very wrong with someone's birth certificate and if there's an indication that this someone used a birth certificate of a newborn child (Virginia Sunahara) who died at birth or soon after birth, we have to talk about the methods Russian intelligence (SVR, a former KGB) and its illegal espionage department. We have to talk about **the illegal spy "documentation process"** - using birth certificates to get legal documents in USA - SS#, driver license, passport.

The Technology
Let's reconstruct Obama's biography as I see it with my 30 years of espionage experience.

63

Illegal spy cover story works best if it's a mix of actual and fake facts. "Obama" (let's call him John Smith) was a child of a student from Kenya who studied in Moscow and dated a Russian girl. Such kids in Russia were often unwanted by both partners and were raised and educated at a special school. Like Obama, John Smith was born in 1961 and, like him, graduated from high school in 1979. KGB paid attention to a very smart young man. Smith was Intelligence Institute student in 1979-1981 in Moscow, not far from "Cosmos" Hotel. There are couple of buildings in the area and I got intelligence education myself in one of them back in 1987, 15 Yaroslavskaya Street, Moscow Russia).

Then a decision was made to train him individually as illegal intelligence officer .The "dacha" (Russian for small villa) not far from Moscow, provides an ideally isolated territory for training.2-3 instructors live there to immerse the candidate completely into his American identity and supervise him all the time. From the first day the candidate becomes accustomed to the circumstances in which he will be living and working in USA for many years. He wears American clothes, eats the food, he's thinking, acting and living like 100% American. He is supplied with newspapers and magazines, he's watching movies and TV shows. The instructors ask the candidate the most difficult questions imaginable. After a number of years of such training, the future illegal knows everything about America, espionage technology and speaks perfect English (by the way, "Obama" once made a very interesting mistake - he said "leave the Agency" instead of "lead the Agency" - watch "Barack Obama 2012: KGB Technology 2008" on YouTube. In espionage business, we say: "One mistake in pronunciation, and the enemy puts a lead dot at the end of the sentence")

After special training the candidate goes through a special process:
   a) Illegal probation period abroad. A trip abroad through intermediate countries with numerous changes of passports and cover stories, jobs, personal connections. Then he gets to the target country, stays there for another

1-2 years and goes back to his country for additional training and correction of cover story — actually, it's his first combat assignment. The most important part of this assignment is to check the reliability of the cover story and documents; the cover story has to be reinforced with new and old true facts, like short-term studies at universities or professional training courses).

b) Intermediate legislation. On his way back the officer could stay in an intermediate country for another 1-2 years, make contacts with business, scientists, government employees, celebrities.

c) Basic legislation. Officer comes to the target country, obtains genuine documents, gets a job which allows him to travel and talk to many people, recruit informants thus creating an illegal station.

At the same time, in 1979-1981, Barack Obama studied at Occidental College in Los Angeles where he became a socialist ready to transform the nation by redistributing wealth. KGB station in Washington, DC which was constantly looking for future secret sources at American top universities and colleges, like Columbia, Yale or Harvard, got information about young socialist. They sent his picture and info to Moscow where some resemblance was discovered between a college student from Los Angeles and a future illegal spy John Smith.

What happened next?

1981

Obama travelled to Indonesia to visit his mother and sister Maya, and visited the families of college friends in India and Pakistan for 3 weeks. Then something happened in India, a good friend to Soviet Union and a perfect place to recruit foreigners. He was recruited and he disappeared.

In Pakistan a poor student who was wearing "thrift store clothing" (from Obama's "Dreams From my Father") managed to stay for 2 weeks and stayed at Lahore Hilton International, was introduced to Yousa Gillani, the Central Working Committee of the Pakistan Muslim League (PML) member and the future prime minister - and went bird-hunting with him. That's exactly what an illegal spy had to do - make business and political contacts on his way to the target country. John Smith aka Barack Obama came back to the United States - change of agents, one of regular illegal espionage methods.

Obama's father, Barack Obama Sr., aged 46 died in a car accident in Nairobi. His mother, Ann Dunham, lived in Indonesia and might be just avoided or ignored by her "son" (Don Johnson, Dunham co-worker, said "Obama was distancing himself from her"). Russians approached her under a "false flag" (National Security Agency or CIA) and explained that her son had to stay abroad for a secret mission for some time. They told her that she had to be ready to accept another person as her own son. For operation like that, espionage agencies often recruit close relatives and allow them to meet their son (daughter) from time to time outside USA. Money talks, there's nothing unusual, though for Dunham the pressure and depression was too big - she died in 1995 of cancer at 52.

Time changes people, so "Obama" had to stay away from his friends and do not show up in public too much.

1981

Same person?

He transferred to Columbia University in New York City, where he majored in political science and where nobody could remember him at all, and graduated with a B.A. in 1983.

"Obama" declined repeated requests to talk about his New York years, release his Columbia transcript or identify a single fellow student, co-worker, roommate or friend from those years. Wall Street Journal editorial in September 2008, titled "Obama's

Lost Years" noted that Fox News contacted 400 of Obama's classmates at Columbia and found no one who even remembered him. "Mostly, my years at Columbia were an intense period of study," Obama told Columbia College Today in a 2005 alumnus interview. "I didn't socialize that much. I was like a monk".

Perfect cover up! Columbia has refused to release any records regarding Obama's attendance, including his application to attend, his grades, and his financial aid records, if any exist. Only one person could order Columbia to shut up - CIA Director Leon Panetta. Why? See next part.

1983-1985
He worked at the Business International Corporation and at the New York Public Interest Research Group. He worked in Chicago as community organizer in 1985-1988.

1987

Barack Obama with his brothers Samson and Ben, Kenya

Question: Who was so important in 1987 that the UK International News Service published his picture?

I have a perfect memory and I state that I saw the man in the center of this picture in Moscow in 1987, where I've been trained at KGB Intelligence Institute.

"Zolotoi Kolos" Hotel, Yaroslavskaya Street 15, Moscow, a secret PGU KGB Intelligence Institute facility. If you open the Moscow hotels catalog, you'll see that this hotel has 5 buildings – 1,3,4,5,7,8 – buildings 2 and 6 "do not exist".

Nearby I saw the man who looked like the person in the center of the picture above in January 1987. I left a small note about that on Internet and on **October 13, 2011** a statement appeared on Internet: *Paul Pieniezny* : "The Obama who was in Russia at that time [1987 – *M.K.*] was not Barack Obama, but a student from Western Africa. He is still alive and well and a diplomat. I have mentioned that little fact a few times on the Fogbow. I hope he sues Mr Kryzhanovsky for every cent he earned in the extreme-right talk circuit". Looks like Obama and his KGb bosses are really scared.

1988
"Obama" travelled to Europe to meet his KGB handlers and get new instructions. He had a choice - a safe variant (to make a political career in one of African countries), and a risky one of staying in America - KGB wanted him to be Martin Luther King #2. But it appeared he could get much more which was Oval Office. It was decided he could stay in USA longer and it was a success: Illinois Senator (1997-2004) and U.S. Senator (2005-2008).

1988-1991

1987   **1988**   **1990**

Same person?

In 1988, Obama entered Harvard Law School. He worked as a summer associate at the law firms of Sidley Austin in 1989 and Hopkins & Sutter in 1990. After graduating from Harvard in 1991, he returned to Chicago.

CHAPTER 2
Mafia Forever

1992

Vyacheslav Ivankov   John DiFronzo   Alexi Giannoulias

Vyacheslav Ivankov ("Yaponchik"), a "Godfather" of Russian mafia came to USA. In 1982 he got 14 years of jail time, was recruited by KGB and got out of jail 5 years earlier, in 1991. He came to USA to build Russian criminal empire, penetrate American economy and political system (Mafia groups in Russia control all big banks and corporations). Victor Sergeev, a former KGB officer, was his adviser.

He was involved in extortion, intimidation, gambling, arms sales, gasoline tax fraud, money laundering. In 1995 FBI recorded his phone call to Moscow: "The base in America is ready"- it was an open threat to the US national security. He was arrested, charged with extortion, got 9 years and then deported to Russia in 2004. In 2009 he was killed by a sniper in Moscow. Ivankov ruled 25 Russian mafia groups in New York, Los Angeles, Miami, Chicago, Boston, Seattle, Detroit and Philadelphia. Russians always make ties to other ethnic crime groups and make deals to avoid gangster wars for territory and influence. Illinois state Russian community is big and rich (around 400,000), that's why Chicago and good relations with the Chicago Outfit boss John DiFronzo were very important for Godfather and KGB asset Ivankov.

I want to know Russian mafia political connections through Chicago mobsters. Why?

Because *New York Post* reported on September 5, 2007:

"A man who has long been dogged by charges that the bank his family owns helped finance a Chicago crime figure will host a Windy City fund-raiser tonight for Sen. Barack Obama. Alexi Giannoulias, who became Illinois state treasurer last year after Obama vouched for him, has pledged to raise $100,000 for the senator's Oval Office bid. Giannoulias bankrolled Michael "Jaws" Giorango, a Chicagoan twice convicted of bookmaking and promoting prostitution. Giannoulias is so tainted by reputed mob links that several top Illinois Dems, including the state's speaker of the House and party chairman, refused to endorse him even after he won the Democratic nomination with Obama's help".

CHAPTER 3
Tom Fife's Adventure

"Last fall, prior to the 2008 presidential election, a friend of mine, Dr. Wiley Drake, former second vice president for the Southern Baptist Convention, sent me an e-mail on which I didn't report. It just seemed too extreme. It was from a software developer he met named Tom Fife who told of how he first heard of the name "Barack".

I can't prove whether it's true or not, but in light of all that is happening, it just doesn't seem that far-fetched anymore. All I know is that Tom Fife is a real guy – not some e-mail scam. I've talked to him. He was a government contractor with an active security clearance who took notes on his trips for debriefings with the Defense Intelligence Agency within the Department of Defense. This is what he wrote down after it happened in 1992, before anyone ever heard the name "Barack":

"During the period of roughly February 1992 to mid-1994, I was making frequent trips to Moscow, Russia, in the process of starting a software development joint-venture company with some people from the Russian scientific community. One of the men in charge on the Russian side was named V. M.; he had a wife named T.M. V. was a level-headed scientist, while his wife was rather deeply committed to the losing Communist cause – a cause she obviously was not abandoning.

One evening, during a trip early in 1992, the American half of our venture were invited to V. & T.'s Moscow flat as we were about to return to the States. The party went well and we had the normal dinner discussions. As the evening wore on, T. developed a decidedly rough anti-American edge – one her husband tried to quietly rein in. The bottom line of the tirade she started against the United States went something like this:

"You Americans always like to think that you have the perfect government and your people are always so perfect. Well then, why haven't you had a woman president by now? You had a chance to vote for a woman vice president and you didn't do it." The general response went something along the lines that you don't vote for someone just because of their sex. Besides, you don't vote for vice president, but the president and vice president as a ticket.

"Well, I think you are going to be surprised when you get a black president very soon."

The consensus we expressed was that we didn't think there was anything innately barring that. The right person at the right time and sure, America would try to vote for the right person, be he or she, black or not.

"What if I told you that you will have a black president very soon and he will be a Communist?"

The out-of-the-blue remark was met by our stares. She continued, "Well, you will; and he will be a Communist."

It was then that the husband unsuccessfully tried to change the subject; but she was on a roll and would have nothing of it. One of us asked, "It sounds like you know something we don't know."

"Yes, it is true. This is not some idle talk. He is already born, and he is educated and being groomed to be president right now. You will be impressed to know that he has gone to the best schools of presidents. He is what you call 'Ivy League.' You don't believe me, but he is real and I even know his name. His name is Barack. His mother is white and American and his father is black from Africa. That's right, a chocolate baby! And he's going to be your president."

She became more and more smug as she presented her stream of detailed knowledge and predictions so matter-of-factly – as though all were foregone conclusions. "It's all been thought out. His father is not an American black, so he won't have that social slave stigma. He is intelligent and he is half white and has been raised from the cradle to be an atheist and a Communist. He's gone to the finest schools. He is being guided every step of the way and he will be irresistible to America."

We sat there not knowing what to say. She was obviously very happy that the Communists were doing this and that it would somehow be a thumbing of their collective noses at America: They would give us a black president and he'd be a Communist to boot. She made it quite obvious that she thought that this was going to breathe new life into world Communism. From this and other conversations with her, she always asserted that Communism was far from dead.

She was full of little details about him that she was eager to relate. I thought that maybe she was trying to show off that this truly was a real person and not just hot air. She rattled off a complete litany. He was from Hawaii. He went to school in California. He lived in Chicago. He was soon to be elected to the Legislature. "Have no doubt: he is one of us, a Soviet." At one point, she related some sort of San Francisco connection, but I didn't understand what the point was and don't recall much about that. I was just left with the notion that she considered the city to be some sort of a center for their activity here.

Since I had dabbled in languages, I knew a smattering of Arabic. I made a comment: "If I remember correctly, 'Barack' comes from the Arabic word for 'Blessing.' That seems to be an odd name for an American." She replied quickly, "Yes. It is 'African,'" she insisted, "and he will be a blessing for world Communism. We will regain our strength and become the number one power in the world." She continued with something to the effect that America was at the same time the great hope and the great obstacle for Communism. America would have to be converted to Communism, and Barack was going to pave the way ".

So, what does this conversation from 1992 prove? Well, it's definitely anecdotal. It doesn't prove that Obama has had Soviet Communist training nor that he was groomed to be the first black American president, but it does show one thing that I think is very important. It shows that Soviet Russian Communists knew of Barack from a very early date. It also shows that they truly believed among themselves that he was raised and groomed Communist to pave the way for their future. This report on Barack came personally to me from one of them long before America knew he existed. Although I had never before heard of him, at the time of this conversation Obama was 30-plus years old and was obviously tested enough that he was their anticipated rising star.

There have been attempts to discredit Fife. He can be reached at: thefife@hotmail.com"
Janet Porter, *WorldNetDaily*, 02.10.2009
1995: Ann Dunham, Obama's mother, aged 52, died of cancer in Honolulu, Hawaii.
1997: Obama was elected the Illinois State Senator
2004: Obama was elected the US Senator.

William Sessions,
FBI Director in 1987-1993, KGB "mole"

Attention:
Obama wasn't afraid to run for the U.S. Senator with his fake identity, his fake birth certificate, fake Social Security # and half-fake biography - why? U.S. Senators get access to top secret documents and all of them must be cleared by FBI. That's why guys with fake ID's never make career in big politics. Obama didn't care - why? Because KGB recruited somebody on the top of FBI hierarchy who covered Obama.

CHAPTER 4
Don't ask Senator Lugar

August 5-7, 2005

Senators Lugar and Obama in Russia

"Obama" visited Russia (together with Senator R. Lugar) and met secretly his SVR (former KGB intelligence) handlers to discuss his prospective for the U.S. presidency. It appeared that U.S. Senator Barack "Obama" was getting out of control and Russians decided to teach him a lesson. Here's what happened.

Sen. Richard Lugar, an Indiana Republican and Chairman of the Senate Foreign Relations Committee, and Sen. Barack Obama, an Illinois Democrat, were detained for three hours on August 7 at an airport in Russia's city of Perm. "We are not certain as to why or the particular activity that caused that delay," Lugar said. He said U.S. Embassy officials informed the senators that "an official at the Foreign Ministry has issued an apology this morning."

No one from the Russian Foreign Ministry could be reached immediately. The U.S Embassy could not immediately confirm the information. Russia's Federal Security Service, however, defended the plane's delay, saying it was because the Perm airport isn't part of an Open Skies Agreement, which allows certain planes to bypass inspections. The FSB, the agency that succeeded the Soviet-era KGB, said it could only comment on the report within a week's time. Maksim Zhalayev, deputy head of the border control service at Perm's airport, accused the senators of refusing to follow border guards' orders, telling Russia's Ekho Moskvy radio that was the reason behind the delay. U.S. Embassy officials said the flight was a U.S. military flight, and therefore should have had diplomatic status. Lugar's spokesman, Andy Fisher, said that Russian officials had initially refused to allow the plane to take off, and insisted on boarding it. "They did not. The border patrol finally got orders to let us go," Fisher said. The senators and their aides spent three days in Russia visiting sites where warheads are stored before destruction under the U.S.-funded Comprehensive Threat Reduction program. This international scandal could never happen without President Putin's straight order.

CHAPTER 5
Gestapo - 2008

February 10, 2007

**Obama" announced his candidacy for
President of the United States**

July 2, 2008
"Obama" made a statement: "We can't rely on our military in order to achieve the national security objectives that we've set. **We got to have a civilian national security force** [like Gestapo - M.K.] **that just as powerful, just as strong, just as well-funded"**. Many Americans, including Congressman Paul Braun, think that Obama wants to establish a Gestapo-like security force to impose a Marxist dictatorship, but I know that he means KGB with its structure and methods – just as I explained in my instructions.

June 6, 2008, Bilderberg Club meeting, Westfields Marriott Hotel, Chantilly, Northern Virginia
Hillary and Obama were invited for the Bilderberg Club meeting. Next day, June 7, Hillary announced she's out of the race. Both Obama and Hillary tried to keep this meeting a secret. Bilderberg Club rules the world and they actually ordered Hillary Clinton to leave the presidential race. *They appointed Obama the President.*

Henry Kissinger is the oldest permanent member of the club and a close friend of Putin, Russian president.

Pelosi "favor"

Barack Obama and Nancy Pelosi

Barack Obama and Joe Biden were nominated as Democratic candidates for the US President and Vice President. House Speaker Nancy Pelosi knew that Obama was not eligible under the US Constitution – that's why she wrote the first variant of nomination certification and then changed it. She deleted "…legally qualified to serve under provision of the United States Constitution…" But before that the House Speaker showed the document to somebody who had enough power to make corrections – who? Her KGB /SVR handler

If she was recruited by KGB – when? Why? How? Money, ideology, career or blackmail?

Now look at the evidence of a federal crime:

Variant 1

DEMOCRATIC NATIONAL COMMITTEE

OFFICIAL CERTIFICATION OF NOMINATION

THIS IS TO CERTIFY that at the National Convention of the Democratic Party of the United States of America, held in Denver, Colorado on August 25 though 28, 2008, the following were duly nominated as candidates of said Party for President and Vice President of the United States respectively and that the following candidates for President and Vice President of the United States are legally qualified to serve under the provisions of the United States Constitution:

For President of the United States

Barack Obama
5046 South Greenwood Avenue
Chicago, Illinois 60615

For Vice President of the United States

Joe Biden
1209 Barley Mill Road
Wilmington, Delaware 19807

Nancy Pelosi
Chair, Democratic National
Convention

Alice Travis Germond
Secretary, Democratic National
Convention

City and County of Denver)
) ss:
State of Colorado)

Subscribed and sworn to before me in the City and County of Denver, State of Colorado, this 28th day of August, 2008.

SHALIFA A. WILLIAMSON
Notary Public
State of Colorado
My Commission Expires September 06, 2011

Notary Public

September 6, 2011
Commission expiration date

Democratic Party Headquarters ■ 430 South Capitol Street, SE ■ Washington, DC, 20003 ■ (202) 863-8000 ■ Fax (202) 863-8174
Paid for by the Democratic National Committee. Contributions to the Democratic National Committee are not tax deductible.
Visit our website at www.democrats.org

Variant 2 – official document

DEMOCRATIC NATIONAL COMMITTEE

OFFICIAL CERTIFICATION OF NOMINATION

THIS IS TO CERTIFY that at the National Convention of the Democratic Party of the United States of America, held in Denver, Colorado on August 25 though 28, 2008, the following were duly nominated as candidates of said Party for President and Vice President of the United States respectively:

For President of the United States

Barack Obama
5046 South Greenwood Avenue
Chicago, Illinois 60615

For Vice President of the United States

Joe Biden
1209 Barley Mill Road
Wilmington, Delaware 19807

Nancy Pelosi
Chair, Democratic National
Convention

Alice Travis Germond
Secretary, Democratic National
Convention

City and County of Denver)
) ss:
State of Colorado   )

Subscribed and sworn to before me in the City and County of Denver, State of Colorado, this 28 day of August, 2008.

SHALIFA A. WILLIAMSON
Notary Public
State of Colorado
My Commission Expires September 06, 2011

Notary Public

September 6, 2011
Commission expiration date

Democratic Party Headquarters ■ 430 South Capitol Street, SE ■ Washington, DC, 20003 ■ (202) 863-8000 ■ Fax (202) 863-8174
Paid for by the Democratic National Committee. Contributions to the Democratic National Committee are not tax deductible.
Visit our website at www.democrats.org.

Attention: KGB Psychotechnologies

Igor Smirnov **Janet Morris**

Igor Smirnov (1950-2004) was a Psychotechnology Research Institute (Moscow) Director, professor, the father of "psychotronic weapons," the Russian term for mind control weapons. His father, Victor Abakumov, was the Minister of State Security (since 1954 - KGB) in 1946-1951. The Institute was established first as KGB psychotechnology lab by KGB Chairman Y. Andropov in 1980.

His research was focused on a unique "psycho-correction" technology - the use of coded acoustic subliminal messages transmitted in "white noise" or music to bend a subject's will, and modify a person's personality without their knowledge. Using an infrasound very low frequency-type transmission, the acoustic psycho-correction message is transmitted via bone conduction - ear plugs would not restrict the message.

Messages like "Vote for Obama!" might be sent through a mobile phone, radio, TV or PC - you don't hear them but your brain accepts them. In a same way the brain accepts the visual image. They by-pass the conscious level and are effective almost immediately.

Janet Morris is President and CEO of M2 Technologies Corp, specializing in non-lethal weapons (NLW), novel technology applications, tactics and technology. Ms. Morris's seminal non-lethal concept and novel technology applications work has been used by the White House Office of Science and Technology Policy. She served at the United States Global

Strategy Council (1989-1994) and at the Center for Strategic and International Studies (1993–1995).

In 1991 Morris met Smirnov who showed her his "Mind Reader". In 1993 Smirnov came to Washington, DC and showed his technology to Bill Clinton's people, Pentagon and CIA experts. In March, 1993 the Richmond, Virginia based Psychotechnologies Corp signed an agreement with Smirnov in which "the Russian side agreed to commit the psycho-correction technologies still in Russia and all related know-how to the US company in exchange for stock. The Russian side has agreed to provide all support necessary to recreate current [psycho-correction] capability in the US and to upgrade the capability using US components and computer programmers. All necessary developmental and existing algorithms will be provided by the Russian side."

In 2008 Barack Obama won presidential elections and it was a national psychosis combined with euphoria. 99% out of 69.5 million Obama's voters can't explain what happened to them and what "CHANGE!" they wanted. Why?

CHAPTER 6
Good Russian Boy

November 4, 2008
Obama won the race and became the first Russian illegal spy to be elected the U.S. President. The Congressional Research Service, a public policy arm of Congress, officially admits no one in the government ever vetted Obama's constitutional eligibility.

November 18, 2008.
After his victory, President "Barack Obama", the most powerful man in the world, lost sense of reality and ignored his Russian intelligence boss (Mikhail Fradkov) instructions - he had his own vision on how to rule and destroy America .Russians were not going to lose control over the White House and American President. They explained to Obama, that it's OK, but he had to work together with Bill Clinton, a "big friend of Russia" and his people. Bill Clinton was instructed what to do and in November 2008 Obama had to divide the power - he appointed Hillary Clinton the Secretary of State, Rahm Emanuel (Clinton's Chief Political Adviser) - the White House Chief of Staff and Leon Panetta (Clinton's Chief of Staff) - CIA Director.

On **October 2, 2010,** he managed to fire Rahm Emanuel (I'll tell you why) and after that Russians humiliated him one more time - in April 28, 2011, he was forced to nominate Panetta to replace Robert Gates as Secretary of Defense. Panetta would end all operations and withdraw all U.S. troops from Iraq - that's another Russian intelligence order. Obama, actually, lost half of his power by giving two key Cabinet positions to Clinton's team - that's how Russians punished their illegal spy for his independence.

And that's what good Russian "Obama" is doing for Russia:
1. He's destroying America – it's called "socialist intervention into the US economy".
A person who wants to spend $1 trillion on health care reform which is not a priority at all in the middle of horrible economic

crisis, in a country with $ 17 trillion national debt is either an idiot or an enemy of America with a very well calculated plan to terminate the country. Obama did it - in March 2010 he signed Health Care Reform legislation into law.

2. He's into **immigration reform which is a socialist intervention into American society** - he'll turn 12 million poor illegal Latinos into US citizens-revolutionaries. In 2014 they'll get green cards, by 2018 they'll get citizenship and bring here all their family members (grandparents, parents, brothers, sisters, brides and grooms) - around 50-60 million unemployed poorly educated people. And that will be the death of America, the end of American Constitution and the birth of a totalitarian "Obama - forever" Communist regime if Hillary Clinton won't stop him.

3. Rising unemployment and inflation, budget deficit at every state and city is another Obama's trick, planned by Russian intelligence - he's pushing big states like Texas, New York and California to a *"boiling point"* after which they might take serious steps towards independence - the beginning of America's death. USSR collapsed the same way - now Russians want revenge using Obama as a hammer.

4. While Bill Clinton saved one Russian "mole" John Deutch, Obama saved 10 (ten) Russian illegal spies, arrested by FBI in June, 2010, sending them back to Russia in 2010 without any investigation - severe blow to American national security and priceless gift to SVR, Russian intelligence. The case is very interesting because Hillary Clinton was the target of Russian spy ring. That's what happened.

Russian spies and American treason
"The President, Vice President and all civil Officers of the United States, shall be removed from Office on Impeachment for, and Conviction of, Treason, Bribery, or other high Crimes and Misdemeanors". **The U. S. Constitution, Article 2, Section 4**

June 28, 2010

FBI arrested in New York, Massachusetts, Virginia and New Jersey 10 Russian illegal spies. All were charged as agents of a foreign government (Russia) and were not registered with the Dept. of Justice, 5 years in jail. Also, all of them except Anna Chapman were charged with conspiracy to commit money laundering, up to 20 years in jail.

In 2007-2010 Alan Patrikof, a financier, a close friend of Clintons, a sponsor Hillary Clinton's election campaigns, had business contacts with vice president of accounting firm "Morea Financial Services, Inc" (120 Broadway, #1016, New York, NY 20271, 212-608-1080) an SVR illegal *Cynthia Murphy (Lydia Gurieva)*. So, the whole group was working for Cynthia Murphy who was trying to get access to Hillary Clinton.

Illegal Russian spy ring: "Cynthia Murphy" – first from the left in the upper row. Alan Patrikof

Philip J. Crowley, assistant press secretary to the US State Department, made right away the statement: *"There is no evidence to suggest that this spy group had U.S. Secretary of State as its principal target".*

"Daily News", 09.30.2010 :"One of the accused Russian sleeper spies may have been trying to worm her way into Secretary of State Clinton's circle of high-powered friends. Suspect Cynthia Murphy worked at a downtown financial firm that appears to have put her in contact with Alan Patricof, a New York venture capitalist and top Democratic donor who was a finance chairman of Clinton's 2008 presidential campaign.The federal complaint states that in February 2009, Murphy reported to Moscow that through work, she had met a financier who was "a personal friend" of a current cabinet official and an active political fund-raiser"

On July 9, 2010 they were exchanged for garbage, 4 defectors convicted in Russia. On July 12 Russian leader, PM Vladimir Putin met the group which was official recognition of their merits. On October 10, 2010, Dmitriy Medvedev, President of Russia, awarded all 10 spies with Russian orders and that means they did a very good job in America destroying its national security.

5. Obama's pro-Russian U.S. National Security Strategy:
"Analysts, agents and officers who protect us must have access to all relevant intelligence throughout the government".
A very dangerous trick – just imagine Russian recruit a "mole" with access to all relevant information.

I call this a *"hologram method".*
If I, Russian "mole", work for CIA as nuclear proliferation analyst, I have access to "all relevant information" throughout US intelligence community: Air Force Intelligence, Army Intelligence, Central Intelligence Agency, Coast Guard Intelligence, Defense Intelligence Agency, Department of Energy, Department of Homeland Security, Department of State Bureau of Intelligence and Research, Department of the Treasury, Drug Enforcement Administration, Federal Bureau of Investigation, Marine Corps Intelligence, National Geospatial-Intelligence Agency , National Reconnaissance Office, National Security Agency Navy Intelligence, Office of Director of National Intelligence

Do you understand what that means? I'll explain. The White House is sending requests for information or research on a certain political or economic problem, situation in Europe, Asia, etc. A "mole' is sending those requests to Moscow and Russians calculate the US strategy, understand? Besides, "mole" is stealing information from all above mentioned agencies. We have to stop it today – just for that deadly blow to American national security Obama has to go to jail as the enemy of state.

6. All his foreign policy actions work for Russia - withdrawal from Afghanistan, withdrawal from Iraq (that's a huge gift for Iran, Russia's best friend), anti-Israel policy (a gift for Palestinian terrorists - Russia's best friends, most of whom were trained in Soviet Union).

7. Obama and World War III.
Russians are the best if it comes to revolutions and SVR, not CIA, is actually behind revolutions in Egypt, Tunisia, Lybia and Syria. Radical Islam comes to power over there + Iran + Palestine and we have a perfect coalition which is ready to start a big war against Israel.

Now, it's extremely important for Russia to re-direct radical Islam vector. It goes through Afghanistan and then through Muslim Turkmenistan, Uzbekistan, Tajikistan and Kazakhstan (former Soviet republics) to Muslim Tatarstan and Muslim Chechnya, constituent republics of Russian federation.
Obama and his Secretary of State Hillary Clinton made numerous statements that USA supports these and other "democratic" revolutions. They protect Russia in such a way and re-direct radicals to USA. Big mistake, Hillary, huge.

Why Russia needs the pro-Russian president of America?
Russia has the world's largest reserves of mineral and energy resources, the world's largest forest reserves and its lakes contain 25% of the world's fresh water. Russia is energy superpower: #1 in the world in natural gas reserves, #8 in oil reserves and #2 in coal reserves.

The sources of energy (oil, gas, uranium, coal) are rapidly coming to an end. At the same time China, India, Brazil, and Indonesia are rapidly growing.

China ranks since 2010 as the world's 2nd largest economy after the US. It became the world's top manufacturer in 2011, surpassing the United States. China is increasing its economy (GDP, gross domestic product) by 10% a year - in 5 years there will be 1,5 China, 1,15 India, 1,5 Brazil ,1,15 Indonesia. 9 billion people on Earth with energy, food and fresh water supplies coming to an end in the next 25-40 years. That means that 500 million Europeans and 300 million Americans have to lower their standards of living - and they will not accept this! On top of it we have the global financial and economic crisis which is actually killing America.

The only way out - to capture resources that still remain to preserve their standards of living.

The World War III is coming - the war between USA and China for Russia's resources. It might start in Middle East and (radical Islam against Israel) and then re-directed to Russia.

Russian leader Putin will do everything and will pay anything to postpone the war as long as possible.

War is coming
November 17, 2010
The 8th annual summit of the Valdai Club closed with a three-hour-long meeting of the summit's participants with the Russian Prime Minister Vladimir Putin, who shared his views on a wide range of issues with the international experts and journalists. Ariel Cohen, senior research fellow at the Heritage Foundation said that Valdai experts discussed a wide range of issues with Putin. Putin did not hesitate to say that *if America continues pursuing its missile defense plans in Europe, serious conflicts may arise in bilateral relations, but Russia is not afraid of this".*

November 8, 2011
Hillary Clinton is pushing Russians to "Arab spring" revolution. She wants to rule the world through my "managed chaos "strategy and KGB asset Obama can do nothing to stop her.

KGB Putin and Hillary

Prime Minister Vladimir Putin strongly criticized U.S. Secretary of State Hillary Rodham Clinton, accusing her of encouraging and funding Russians protesting 2011 State Duma election fraud, and warned of a wider Russian crackdown on dissent. By describing Russia's parliamentary election as rigged, Putin said Clinton "gave a signal" to his opponents.

"They heard this signal and with the support of the U.S. State Department began their active work," Putin said in televised remarks. He said the United States is spending "hundreds of millions" of dollars to influence Russian politics with the aim of weakening a rival nuclear power.

Putin's tough words show the deep cracks in U.S.-Russian ties despite President Barack Obama's efforts to "reset" relations with the Kremlin.

Putin warned that the government might take an even harder line against those who try to influence Russia's political process on behalf of a foreign government. He accused the U.S. State Department of spending "hundreds of millions" of dollars in Russia and his government has to "work out ways to protect our sovereignty from outside interference." "We are the largest nuclear power," Putin said, addressing supporters during a televised meeting. **"And our partners have certain concerns and shake us so that we don't forget who is the master of this planet, so that we remain obedient and feel that they have leverage to influence us within our own country."** He said "especially unacceptable is the infusion of foreign money into the electoral process."

It's interesting that Hillary Clinton's #1 supporter is Republican Senator John McCain who said on October 20, 2011: "I think dictators all over the world, maybe even Mr. Putin, maybe some Chinese, maybe all of them should be a little bit more nervous because the people of Libya rose up. We assisted them and if it hadn't been for the British and French, NATO air power, they probably wouldn't have succeeded. I think they are to be nervous. I think it's the spring, not just Arab spring. I can't predict it – armed uprising or anything like that – but I can certainly see significant protest in a lot of countries.

April, 2011
"Barack Obama" announced his intention to seek re-election in 2012.

CHAPTER 7
How CIA Was Killing Me

Dr. Jeffrey M. Bernstein, CIA assassin,
who had to kill me, cardiologist at North Shore
University Hospital in Manhasset, New York.

December 24, 2010, Christmas Eve
This day, around 3pm. I had a very strong chest pain and had to call the ambulance. They took me to ER (emergency room) at North Shore University Hospital in Manhasset, New York, one of the best in New York State as they explained to me. I was admitted to the hospital around 7pm and Dr. Jeffrey Bernstein, cardiologist, talked to me for 10 minutes and left. My blood pressure was high; I asked the nurse for the medication and she informed me that Bernstein had decided to cut my Atenolol (medication for high blood pressure) in half – from 0.5 mg a day to 0.25 mg. He said that too much Atenolol was making me dizzy. I asked her to call the doctor and give me my full dose. She gave me half and promised to find the doctor.

My blood pressure was still high and slowly it started to grow. I called the nurse, she took my blood pressure, told me she couldn't find the doctor and left. In 5 minutes my heart was pumping like crazy, I had horrible headache and dizziness, the pressure was, probably more than 200/120, then it grew higher.

I got out of the bed and left the room, though I could hardly walk. **There was nobody at cardiology, not a single person – all of them disappeared. There was dead silence**.

Very strange. I got back to my bed and pressed the button, calling the nurse – nothing happened. Finally, the nurse came and I asked her to take me to emergency room to get my medication before I die. She said that it's against the rules, I have to calm down, though they still couldn't find Bernstein, and she left.

I was dying, but I didn't want to die. I've grabbed big plastic cup with water, threw it out of the room to make noise and attract someone's attention, and fainted. I was lucky – some nurse heard the noise, though CIA did everything to clean up the whole floor until I have a stroke or heart attack.

I saw around ten people when I opened my eyes – there were guys from ER holding my electrocardiogram – it was horrible. I got my pill and Bernstein came in half an hour, obviously surprised that I was alive.

CHAPTER 8
Here Comes Hillary

2016 is coming and there's a player who'll never give up and whom Russian intelligence service can't stop. Hillary Clinton, a former US Secretary of State, with a team of her own.

March, 2010
I've received an invitation for a dinner with President Obama and Speaker of the House Pelosi from DCCC (Democratic Congressional Campaign Committee) signed by Ian Sugar, Director of Development. Sugar explained that I pay $15,999 (credit card) and on May 13, 2010 at 6.00 PM I had to come to St. Regis Hotel, New York.

Event Chair
The Honorable Steve Israel, The Honorable Eliot L. Engel, The Honorable Nita M. Lowey, The Honorable Jerrold Nadler, The Honorable Gregory W. Meeks, The Honorable Joseph Crowley, The Honorable Anthony Weiner, The Honorable Scott Murphy along with Members of the New York Congressional Delegation along with Nancy Pelosi, SPEAKER OF THE HOUSE and Chris Van Hollen, CHAIRMAN OF THE DEMOCRATIC CONGRESSIONAL CAMPAIGN COMMITTEE Invite you to join President Barack Obama Thursday, May 13, 2010

St. Regis Hotel Ballroom, Two East 55th Street at Fifth Avenue, New York, New York
6:00 p.m. – Host Committee VIP Reception
6:30 p.m. – Dinner
For more information or to RSVP, please contact
Diana Fassbender at 202-485-3438 or diana@dccc.org

Host: write/raise $50,000 per couple (Includes Host Committee VIP Reception, Presidential Photo and Dinner)

Guest: $15,000 per person / $30,000 per couple (Includes Presidential Photo and Dinner)
I cannot attend but enclosed is my contribution of $ _____
Please make checks payable to the "DCCC" and mail to:
Speaker Nancy Pelosi, 430 South Capitol Street SE, Second Floor, Washington, DC 20003

If you would like to contribute by credit card please complete the following and return via fax to (202) 478-9499 or http://www.dccc.org/PresidentObamaNYC.
Please charge my personal credit card $ _____

May 13, 2010 Paid for by the Democratic Congressional Campaign Committee.
430 South Capitol Street, SE • Washington, DC 20003 • (202) 863-1500 •

Now, guess who was the DCCC Chairman in 2005-2009 and who could advise Ian Sugar to send Kryzhanovsky, a former KGB sniper, an invitation to a dinner with Obama? Rahm Emanuel. I didn't go; instead I wrote a letter to Obama to show vulnerability of his protection system.

All I had to do was:
> **buy 9mm Zig Zauer practice to get used to the pistol, come to St. Regis unarmed, disarm any Secret Service pig and complete the job**

October 12, 2010

Mark Sullivan, US Secret Service Director in 2006-2013

CIA, FBI and Secret Service wanted me to play Oswald #2. And then what?

I had a meeting with two Secret Service agents, John and Bratt (646-842-2107). It appeared that 2 teams were hunting me all over New York City because I "talk too much". They explained to me that I "was a very lucky guy" because John and Bratt (team #1) found me, not team # 2 which might "treat me much worse".

I said: "If you want to kill me, put sniper in a house across the street - I'm not scared". They had no comments on that but they got very nervous when I mentioned the word "murder". We had a long discussion. I've asked them why they allow the White House press office to put Obama's next day schedule on Internet with exact time and place of his trips - it gives a perfect possibility to kill him. They told me it was Rahm Emanuel's order and they can do nothing though on October 2, 2010 Obama fired Emanuel and it was a small victory over Clintons. More interesting - they told me they wanted me to work for them too". We are not here to kill you. We know you as "Filament", you work for CIA and we want you to work for us too under the same alias. We'll pay you". So, I'm still acting CIA agent and they're still sure I'll do political murders? And who's the target - Obama? That's why Secret Service is nervous - they are in the game?

Before that, team # 2, two men and a woman armed with handguns, found my family in Brooklyn, interrogated them in a very rude manner, illegally searched the apartment, took PC and kept it for a month, and ordered my wife and son not to tell me about their visit in case I make a phone call. It looks like Secret Service Director Mark Sullivan (retired in 2013) didn't make a final decision yet - to kill me or not.

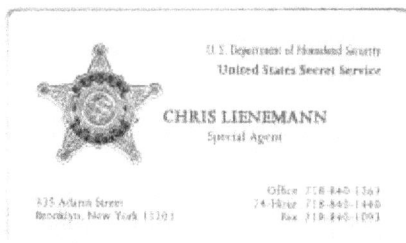

Team #2 business cards

Team #2 members who were ready to kill me:
Chris Lienemann, special agent, tel. 718-840-1263
Susan Klemm, special agent, tel. 718-840-1448
Gene Gurevich, special agent, tel. 718-840-1305
Address: 335 Adams Street, 30th floor, Brooklyn, NY 11201

That's not the end.

January, 20 2011

Obama and FBI Director Robert Mueller

**CIA Director Panetta & Secretary of State Hillary Clinton.
His promotion to Defense Secretary was a "miracle"**

I talked for about one hour to FBI agent Eric Perry, Queens, NY field office, 80-02 Kew Gardens Road Kew Gardens, NY 11415. Phone: (718) 286-7100). He informed me that my letter made "high authorities, people on the very top are extremely nervous". He didn't explain if it was FBI Director Robert Mueller or the White House Chief of Staff. Why FBI is so nervous, they are in the game?

Like with JFK assassination, you don't need huge conspiracy - it's enough if CIA Director John Brennan, FBI Director James Comey and Secret Service Director Julia Pierson make a deal - simple, right, Mrs. Hillary Clinton? I still keep your letters where you promise any help. I ask you not to kill "Barack Obama", even if he's a fake President and you know it, and he's your personal enemy. You can make a deal - he'll resign and go back to Russia, and you take the Oval Office, nice and quiet.

No matter what people might think and say, Obama is a spy - my 30 years of experience, my knowledge of espionage business, my intuition, his behavior, his aggressive style, his manner to talk and treat people (he's never asking - he's always ordering) - everything says he's my brother in arms, Russian intelligence officer, and **he was t r a i n e d to be the U.S. President.** Tell Brennan, Comey and Pierson to leave him alone. No bullet, no staged car accident, no "heart attack", please.

Operations like these leave no witnesses. Once Obama was elected the US President, there are only 2 guys who know the truth about him in Russia – Russian President Putin and SVR Director Fradkov.

Putin and Obama

And 3 more guys who know everything about Obama in the States:

- Bill Clinton who blackmailed him in November 2008 and forced him to take his people
- a former CIA Director Leon Panetta who was "promoted" to Defense Secretary without any explanation
- a former FBI Director Robert Mueller (Obama is scared of him to death - violated the law and asked the Congress 2 more years for Mueller)

Who are these last two to be treated like kings by Obama? Nobodys who could blackmail him.

So, let's explain "Millennium Hilton" first, smell the court and jail, and then maybe they can make a deal and talk about Obama ?

I think that's a good suggestion and it has to be published - they have to move after that, deny, make statements. It's good - once they start talking, you cut every answer in small pieces (episodes) and ask questions on each. It's gonna be very hard to lie then.

I'm "the most dangerous man" in America

Do I look #1 U.S. wanted?

September 10, 2011

I had a chat with a very professional "somebody" on Internet, here's a report.

- I did some digging.....you're on the FBI, CIA, NSA [National Security Agency – M.K.], and even DIA [Defense Intelligence Agency – M.K.] top 25 watch list....don't worry, I have this page secured, but damn, did you know this?

- How you got it?

- Well I didn't find it on Wiki! I had to hack, do some "overtime" work in the office, wasn't supposed to, but did it anyway.

- Can I see this info?

- I didn't dare lift it.

- Most interesting is DIA.

- Not really. You'd be surprised, the USA intelligence community is a mess, everybody does everybody else work, and does it badly.

- True.

- Interns can view classified files from work without anyone noticing, it's pathetic that I did what I just did, I shouldn't have been able to but I could.

- Still, I'd like to know what DIA wants.

- I have no idea why they find you a subject of such high interest.

- They erased 3 days ago YouTube "Barack Obama 2012: KGB Technology 2008".
- Ex KGB officer living in the United States. I'd say with all you've done, I'm surprised you're not on EVERY list.
- So, can I have a look?
- I haven't done any lifts yet, as long as you don't "touch" anything, it's harder to trace, and I'll see what I can do. I'll get back to you.

So, National Security Agency and Defense intelligence Agency is involved in anti-American conspiracy too? CIA, FBI, Secret Service, NSA and Pentagon? What's going on, America? What's going on, DIA Director Lieutenant General Ronald Burgess and NSA Director General Keith Alexander? What's going on, America?

November 22, 2013
President Obama said that although the tragedy transformed the U.S. Secret Service [after JFK assassination - M.K.], which protects him and his family today; he doesn't spend much time worrying about his personal safety. "It's not something I think about," Obama told ABC News' Barbara Walters in an interview . "Mainly because *we have a Secret Service that does an outstanding job every single day.*"

"Dead drop" in Canberra - Hillary?
November 18, 2011
A booklet detailing Barack Obama's security arrangements during his Australian visit this week has been found lying in a gutter in Canberra, the Australian capital.

The Sydney Morning Herald, whose reporter happened upon the booklet - titled "Overall Program and Orders of Arrangements: Program for the State Visit to Australia by President of the United States Barack Obama" — considers it "a significant and hugely embarrassing security slip-up."

It quotes security analyst, Alan Dupont, as saying the booklet's loss represented a significant security breach:

"If that had got into the wrong hands it would certainly put the President and some of his entourage at risk, if someone could respond quickly enough to having the information," said Dupont, from Sydney University. "Even if you were an ordinary crime, there would be a market for that kind of book, so it's not good news."

The booklet describes Obama's Australian schedule "down to the minute, as well as the breakdown of his security convoy, and the mobile numbers of dozens of senior US and Australian officials," the SMH reported.

The cover of the 125-page booklet even reads: "is not to be communicated either directly or indirectly to any person not authorized to receive it."

The booklet names a long-standing member of the Secret Service and details seating arrangements for the presidential motorcade, even describing from which limousine door the President will enter and exit.

It also describes his security convoy, locating the "counter-assault teams," a "comms vehicle," an "intel car," and the "hammer truck." Hammer stands for "hazardous agent mitigation medical emergency response."

Looks like it was a dead drop operation. The question is – who "dropped" the classified Secret Service booklet and for whom? Who wanted to kill Obama in Australia? Question for you, Mrs. Hillary Clinton.

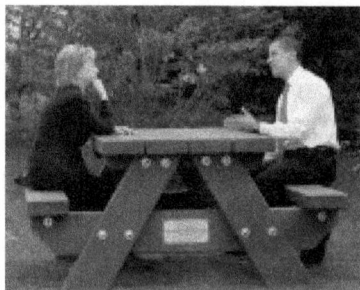

What U.S. Secret Service agents do instead of protecting the U.S. President

April 14, 2012, Cartagena, Colombia

12 Secret Service agents have been sent home from the Summit of the Americas here this weekend because of allegations of "misconduct," U.S. officials said late Friday. The agents were relieved of duty at the summit and replaced with new agents.

It happened prior to President Obama's arrival in Colombia. The incident involved suspicion of involvement with a prostitute by at least one of the agents who refused to pay her $800 and gave $30.

The matter is being handled by the Secret Service's Office of Professional Responsibility, its internal affairs division. Although Colombia permits prostitution in certain "tolerance" areas, its solicitation would be considered inappropriate at all times by the Secret Service. Several of the agents involved in the incident are married, according to the Post.

November 15, 2013

Agents and supervisors of the US Secret Service have engaged in misconduct in 17 countries in recent years, *The Washington Post* reported. It quoted accounts given by whistleblowers to a Senate committee that oversees the Secret Service. These accounts contradict assertions by Secret Service leaders that the agency does not tolerate sexually improper behavior, Senator Ronald Johnson, the top Republican on a Homeland Security subcommittee, said Thursday, the Post reported. The Post said two people briefed on the accounts said they include agents and managers hiring prostitutes and visiting brothels during official trips. They also allegedly had extramarital affairs on the road, and had one-night stands or long-term relationships with foreign nationals that were not properly reported, the Post said. The Post said one whistleblower told the paper that senior management was aware of agents hiring prostitutes on foreign and domestic trips. One of those disciplined, Ignacio Zamora, had led an internal probe into a scandal last year in which more than a dozen Secret Service agents drank and caroused with prostitutes ahead of a presidential visit for an international summit in the city of Cartagena. The Secret Service learned of Zamora's e-mails to the subordinate after he tried to retrieve a bullet that he had left behind in a woman's room at the posh Hay-Adams hotel near the White House, the Post says

Bonus

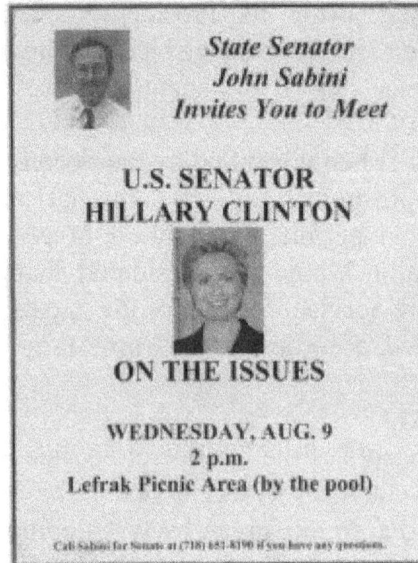

State Senator
John Sabini
Invites You to Meet

**U.S. SENATOR
HILLARY CLINTON**

ON THE ISSUES

WEDNESDAY, AUG. 9
2 p.m.
Lefrak Picnic Area (by the pool)

Call Sabini for Senate at (718) 651-8190 if you have any questions.

August 9, 2006
At 8 A.M. I saw strange green flyers inside the Lefrak City, Queens, NY, buildings saying that: "State Senator John Sabini invites you to meet U.S. Senator Hillary Clinton on the issues. Lefrak City (by the pool). Wednesday, August 9, 2 P.M. Call Sabini for Senate at 718-651-8190 if you have any questions".

Ok. Do you know what's Lefrak City? It's 20 old brick 18-floor projects for poor African-Americans, Latinos, and Russians. The most dangerous area in Queens and the New York State, stuffed with street gangs, crack cocaine, heroin, prostitutes and illegal guns. Recently 100 NYPD officers stormed the ghetto and arrested 13 most ruthless gangsters who terrorized people for years (another 10 are still wanted), confiscated guns, ammunition, drugs and $2.5 million in cash. On August 1, 2006 NYS Senator John Sabini delivered a speech at Lefrak City community meeting at St. Paul's Church demanding new, severe state and federal laws to control illegal weapons. And now, the same Sabini invites everybody to meet in person a former First Lady, the U.S. Senator Hillary Clinton at some open playground. What's that? A sweet candy for terrorists? A regular stupidity?

I saw flyers at 8 A.M., and in two minutes I was already walking to the place – just to make sure Mrs. Clinton will meet the voters guarded by the "best of the best" – the U.S. Secret Service.

I was sure they already watch the area for the last 24 hours.

I was sure the access to the area is restricted.

I was sure that one week before the event local police instructed the secret sources to stay at alert and report any suspicious activity and people who had or tried to purchase illegal guns.

I was sure bad guys and aggressive psychos were isolated temporarily or kept under control at least.

I was sure technicians checked the air, soil and water (in the open pool) for radioactivity and toxic substances, looked for explosives and brought a specially trained dog.

I was sure there was no access to a single roof and they've installed a metal detector to check VIP and other guests.

I was sure they had a double checked guest list. Kill me, I was sure the Secret Service would never let any bad guy approach Hillary Clinton. I was wrong.

At 8.30 A.M. I was there. Nothing. Nobody.

The place was a heaven for terrorists:
- a circle of six 18-floor-1500-window buildings (such meetings in the open areas close to residential buildings are strictly forbidden for people guarded by Secret Service)
- a playground
- an open stage under a small roof (no walls)
- a barbeque place
- a pool

And 6 hours to get ready for assassination:
- observe the place and then plan assassination –
- install a mine under a stage
- try a silenced sniper rifle out of any window or from the roof and make necessary corrections if there any bullet deviations
- bring and place the whole army of terrorists all over the place

At 11 A.M. two girls, three assistants and free "Pepsi" appeared out of nowhere. 2 cops – in and out. No restriction. Not even a "Don't cross" tape.

At 1 P.M. about 500 people came to the playground – retired old men and women, homeless alcoholics, drug addicts, kids, teens and reporters.

At 2.30 P.M. people surrounded the playground and screamed like crazy when Hillary Clinton finally appeared among them and tried to make her way through the crowd. Anybody could touch or hit her - 2 cops and 2 Secret Service agents just smiled. Then she got to the stage encircled by a wild, absolutely uncontrolled crowd. One agent was standing behind her, another one – at the stairs. No security. I had to move close to the stage – the situation was unpredictable and I could help to protect Mrs. Clinton with my "The Nabat" KGB anti-terror group experience.

She made a 15 minutes speech and then I witnessed a total chaos – still on the stage, she tried to shake hands and people went wild; somebody gave her flowers (absolutely unacceptable thing), somebody asked her to hold a baby to take pictures; people screamed and pushed each other. I had to ask people to move back and some did. I was at the stage, right at the middle and people couldn't reach Hillary Clinton easily, some women tried to push me - I was playing a nice guy, but didn't leave my spot.

Agents paid no attention – they were chewing gums, obviously proud of their James Bond style sunglasses. Poor Sabini asked people to move away – nobody cared. Only when some young girls jumped up on the stage, police officer reluctantly restricted the place with a yellow tape – the Secret Service guy looked at him surprised. Then Hillary turned over to talk to somebody on the stage, and the agent turned his back to the crowd – I couldn't believe it.

At 3.30 she left the playground and had to move through the huge crowd again. I was next to her pretending I'm making video. She was lucky - God saved her and I helped him a little bit.

CHAPTER 9

"National crisis" – mission not accomplished

September 8, 2011
US national debt is $17 trillion.
In 2009 Obama pushed through an $800 billion economic stimulus package.
In 2010 - $1 trillion health care reform, "Obamacare"
In 2011, November 8 - he asked the Congress to pass $447 billion "American Jobs Act" and declared that the country, the **United States of America is in** *"national crisis"*.

(KGB instructions for Obama, "The Professional" by M. Kryzhanovsky
Crisis
Crisis means that your government as a system is exhausted and it's unable to rule the nation and resources effectively in an extreme situation, including economic, natural catastrophes and war. A crisis has three stages:
1) before the crisis, when the first signs appear
2) crisis development until culmination
3) catastrophe followed by impeachment
A crisis could be programmed at the very beginning of your term (mistakes in political and economic courses, inexperienced personnel, faulty planning) or it can appear later (too many mistakes, change of political environment, shifts in the economic or international situation).

What I want
1. US Congress and Department of Justice full investigation into US President Barack Obama, Bill Clinton, CIA Directors since 1995, a FBI Director Robert Mueller and a former US Secret Service Director Mark Sullivan anti-American conspiracy.

2. Compensation for 10 years of sufferings, poverty and homelessness. I'll spend the money to build up a private national security agency to protect America.

3. CIA has to be terminated. FBI and Secret Service – reformed.

4. **De-obamafication of America**

WHAT WE HAVE:
1) President who is the enemy of state
2) Disabled White House administration
3) Paralyzed House and Senate
4) 14 million unemployed people out of 150 million which is 9.1%
5) National debt of $17 trillion which will never be paid off
6) Coming hungry revolution.

WHAT WE HAVE TO DO:
1) Understand:
   - that there are no more Democrats and Republicans - there are Patriots and Communists
   - that we, people , hire the President, Senators and Representatives as top political managers, and we have the power to fire them.

2) "Obama Has to Resign" state referendums.

3) Define Red States (Utah, Idaho, Wyoming, Nebraska, Alaska, Oklahoma, Kansas, North Dakota, Alabama, Texas, Mississippi, South Dakota, South Carolina, Montana, Kentucky, Indiana, Georgia, North Carolina, Tennessee, Arizona, Louisiana, Virginia) as Patriotic States.

4) Create the Patriotic States Union (PSU). The US states governors, members of the Union Council, have to sign the Declaration, giving the state's economic independence. Union will be open to any Blue or Purple (swing) state.

5) De-Obamafication of America.
Every state has to protect itself from Obama's war against America. Communist and any other anti-American activity, including pro-Obama propaganda in the Union has to be

abolished. President Obama's physical access to the Union states has to be blocked, his election offices - closed. All present laws signed by Obama have to be cancelled if they work against people.

6) Declare state of emergency in the Union to fix wages and food prices.

7) Amend Constitution to make sure that Communists and Fascists will never get to the Oval Office again.

Jeh Johnson, US Secretary of Homeland Security also involved in anti-American conspiracy. His most important "immigration" job – to press and blackmail me to get me back as assassin.

December 8, 2011
"Mr. Kryzhanovsky, We can do nothing about CIA. **National security is not our business**". Michael Eatroff, Constituent Liaison, Office of Senator Kirsten Gillibrand, 780 Third Avenue, Suite 2601,New York, (212) 909-0492 (Phone).

U.S. Senator Kirsten Gillibrand, (D), NY

On November 9, John from NYPD Anti-Terror Dept called me and said that Michael Eatroff from Senator Kristine Gillibrand's office informed them that I wanted to kill Gillibrand. He asked me who I am and if I really wanted to kill the Senator. I told him I'm "Filament' and I have problems with CIA, not with Gillibrand. John was shocked to hear that I'm "Filament", he said "it changes everything, I know about you a lot".

He wanted to meet me right away, because, as he said "we are brothers" (I was KGB "Nabat" anti-terror group sniper), but then we changed it to Tuesday, after his morning call – he said "at your favorite pizzeria, Mike".
He didn't call on Tuesday, November 13.

What does that mean:
1. He saw a classified document at Anti-Terror Dept about "Filament", saying I'm a professional spy and a sniper, "not to be touched". Anti-Terror NYPD Dept. is watching me.

2. I'm "untouchable' and that means CIA wants to set me up the same way they used Oswald ("passive sabotage").

3. They might do something bad to somebody in NYC, where I live, and it might be just a fake attempt followed by my arrest or murder. I'm a former KGB – they might blame Russia for it – the smell of war between Russia and USA is in the air, Hillary Clinton and Senator McCain are talking about coming Russian revolution, Putin said at "Valdai" Club meeting that Russia might terminate USA in less than half an hour.

4. I'm RNC platinum member, I have a support letter from Bush – they might blame Republicans for it.

5. The operation might be a huge promo for Obama's campaign if Obama is behind this. It might happen in January-February, so they could talk about it the whole year.

6. John wanted to see me Tuesday because he wanted to get instructions from hiss Chief. On Monday they told John to shut up and forget about "Filament".

January 9, 2012
Obama kicked Bill Clinton's guy off the White House. Bill Daley, a former President Bill Clinton's Secretary of Commerce, resigned as Obama's Chief of Staff.

CHAPTER 10
Watch the Microphone!

March 20, 2012
Barack Obama "pushed" me to add this chapter – about the unexpected punch to his KGB/SVR spy career. Like one of my Moscow Intelligence Institute said: "Mike, remember, one mistake in pronunciation and you'll get a nice tiny bullet in your smart head!" Let's see what happened and how KGB "Barack Obama" operation nearly came to its end.

Barack Obama and Russian President Dmitriy Medvedev,

Obama-Medvedev Secret Talk Decoded by Mikhail Kryzhanovsky
Seoul, March 26, 2012
Obama and Russian President Medvedev had a short talk before press conference, unaware that the microphone was on.

I can decode this talk between SVR (Russian Intelligence) asset Obama and one of his handlers, Medvedev, - the other one is Vladimir Putin, Russian President-elect since 03.04.2012.

The secret deals.
"On these issues, but particularly missile defense, this can be solved, but it's important for him [Putin] to give me space".
Barack Obama.

Explanation.
1) "...these issues can be solved".
Obama promised that America won't start war in Iran in 2012 and, for sure, it won't happen after Obama is re-elected. Obama

and Medvedev reached a secret deal on Iranian nuclear program, because Obama didn't even mention it; it's a minor problem now.
2) "...particularly missile defense...this can be solved"
Obama and Medvedev already reached a secret deal on American missile defense in Europe - Obama will put it on hold until 2016, for the period of his future second term.
3) "It's important for him [Putin] to give me space"
Obama didn't mention Putin's name and that means that secret deals in Seoul were initiated by Putin, not
Medvedev. Obama is begging Putin to "give him space" and that means Putin is pressing Obama hard as his asset.

Dmitriy Medvedev: *"Yes, I understand. I understand your message about space. Space for you..."*

Explanation.
Medvedev didn't promise to stop pressure, he promised "understanding".
That means: "We understand you can't be weak on these issues now. But Putin, who's not as strong and popular in Russia as before, wants to start his presidency with international victory - missile defense in Europe is a threat to Russia and it has to be removed".

Barack Obama: *"This is my last election. After my election I have more flexibility".*

Explanation.
Obama is 100% sure he's re-elected and that means Obama and Medvedev reached a secret deal on Obama's 2012 campaign financing.
"After my election I have more flexibility" means "If Russian intelligence could finance my campaign properly, I'll get the second term and you'll get whatever you want, but not before".

Dmitriy Medvedev: *"I understand. I will transmit this information to Vladimir [Putin] and I stand with you".*

Explanation.
1) Again, Medvedev promised "understanding" and that means that Putin will make ultimate decision on Obama's campaign financing.
2) "Transmit", "transmitter" is espionage technical jargon. Medvedev would never use it if it was a regular meeting of two presidents. He would rather say "I'll inform Putin on that"

Why it happened.
1. Unlike Putin, who was a professional spy, Medvedev is just a former lawyer.
2. Obama and Medvedev lost a sense of reality; otherwise they wouldn't talk without complete privacy.

Who's America's enemy?

November 24, 2011
Russian Resident Dmitry Medvedev:
"First, I am instructing the Defense Ministry to immediately put the missile attack early warning radar station in Kaliningrad on combat alert. Second, protective cover of Russia's strategic nuclear weapons, will be reinforced as a priority measure under the program to develop out air and space defenses. Third, the new strategic ballistic missiles commissioned by the Strategic Missile Forces and the Navy will be equipped with advanced missile defense penetration systems and new highly-effective warheads. Fourth, I have instructed the Armed Forces to draw up measures for disabling missile defense system data and guidance systems if need be... Fifth, if the above measures prove insufficient, the Russian Federation will deploy modern offensive weapon systems in the west and south of the country, ensuring our ability to take out any part of the US missile defense system, in Europe".

"We can terminate the USA in less than half an hour". V. Putin, PM of Russia, elected President of Russia on 03.04.2012
June 29, 2012

I've contacted on CIA - FBI- US Secret Service conspiracy Office of Inspector General of the Intelligence Community, Washington, DC 20511703-482-1300, ICIG_Complaints@dni.gov

William Shea, williams1@dni.gov:
"Michael, I have received and read all four emails. However, I still see no proof of any connection to the CIA, and you have not explained how the CIA is affecting your life at this time. What is happening to you that you want to have stopped?

My answer:
"Bill, Inspector General of the Intelligence Community has to ask CIA Director David Petraeus why and how I, a former KGB spy, got immigration status in America. Then you'll open investigation into the conspiracy.

June 30, 2012
William Shea: **"CIA told me that "Filament" doesn't exist".**

July 30, 2012

DEPARTMENT OF HOMELAND SECURITY			
United States Secret Service			
NAME Mykhaylo Kryzhanovsky	DATE OF BIRTH 11/12/58	SOCIAL SECURITY NUMBER ███████	
ADDRESS No perm. address			
(signature)			
SIGNATURE			DATE 07.31.2012
SIGNATURE OF WITNESS *(signature)*	NAME OF WITNESS SA Pietramica		DATE 7/31/12
TITLE / AGENCY OF WITNESS SA / USSS			
SIGNATURE OF GUARDIAN	NAME OF GUARDIAN		DATE

I had a meeting with another Secret Service agent again. This time – with Jason Pietramica and Tim (718-840-1000), who asked me again if I, a former KGB sniper, can and if I want to

116

kill President Obama. Then, they asked another question – if I can go to Russia. A former KGB spy and a sniper is being asked to go to Russia? For what? *Obama wants to get rid of Russian President Putin, his boss? I mean, kill him. And they want me again?*

Looks like Secret Service has to define its priorities, though they didn't as me to do anything right away – they just asked me questions. I said I can go if there's a job for me; otherwise I have nothing to do there. They didn't explain what they wanted; they just were interested if I was ready to do a "job" in Russia.

But why they asked about Obama? Who's interested this time? I couldn't find the answer until the news about problems inside Obama's family appeared.

January 11, 2014, Washington, D.C.

Barack and Michelle Obama are going through a severe marital crisis, which reached its peak after photographs were taken of Obama flirting with the head of the Danish government during the memorial ceremony of Nelson Mandela. She yelled at her husband because she is "tired of it". Michelle is waiting for her husband to end his second term in order not to damage his political career and then she will implement the separation process. The couple is sleeping in separate rooms in the White House. Michelle turned to a divorce lawyer to handle the matter, in order to ensure that she will receive half of their shared property. An official in Washington even appraised that the couple will end their relationship and that it appears like a "sure bet."

One more thing. She might get the information about his cooperation with Russian intelligence.

From whom? Hillary Clinton? Why not

CHAPTER 11
Operation in Progress: Four More Years

November 6, 2012
Obama was re-elected

Operation is still in progress. Look:
1. February 11, 2012, Washington, DC, Department of State
U.S. Sen. John Kerry (D -Mass.) took the ceremonial oath of office for the position of Secretary of State. The swearing in, administered by Vice President Joe Biden, finalized the transition of power in the Department of State from former Secretary of State Hillary Clinton to Kerry. *So, Obama fired, finally, the worst of Russia's enemy - Hillary Clinton.*

2. February 11, 2013, Washington, D.C.
White House officials are looking at a cut that would take the arsenal of deployed weapons to just above 1,000. Currently there are about 1,700, and the new strategic arms reduction treaty with Russia that passed the Senate at the end of 2009 calls for a limit of roughly 1,550 by 2018.

Questions exist as to how to accomplish such a reduction considering that Republicans in the Senate opposed even the modest cuts in the new arms reduction treaty, called Start, according to the New York Times. The White House is loath to negotiate an entirely new treaty with Russia, which would lead to Russian demands for restrictions on American and NATO missile-defense systems in Europe and would reprise a major fight with Republicans in the Senate over ratification.

3. February 12, 2012, Washington, DC, Obama's State of the Union
SVR, Russian intelligence helped Obama to be elected the US President. It was a very smart operation, *because politically correct Congress can't stop a black president from destroying* America. Being re-elected, Obama declared himself a Communist in his State of Union on February 12, 2013: "If you

make more than $1 million a year, you should not pay less than 30 percent in taxes. **Now, you can call this class warfare all you want**".

Besides, that's what he said about Iran: "**America [Obama-M.K.] is determined to prevent Iran from getting a nuclear weapon, and I will take no options off the table to achieve that goal**".

I have to explain what's going on. Russia pushed Obama to use the "controlled chaos strategy" through radical Muslims - that's why they are coming to power after Arab spring revolutions in Tunisia, Egypt, Libya plus Syria in the nearest future. Very soon the whole Muslim world will be against America. So, Obama is helping Russia to start war "Muslims against the USA". I call it treason. According to Constitution the President might be impeached for the treason.

4. February, 23, 2013, Moscow, Kremlin

Russian President Vladimir Putin is happy with his asset "Obama". He made the following statement: "We plan to upgrade 70 percent of all main types of weapons by 2020. Naturally we will accomplish this by drawing on the strengths of our national defense industry. We will rely on national industry and design centers, into which huge funds are being invested in order to accomplish the above goals".

5. February 25, 2013

"Time to Invest in Russia?" TopForeignStocks.com by David Hunkar from David Hunkar Consulring LLC.

"The best way to invest in Russian equities is via the Market Vectors Russia ETF (RSX). This fund has about 42% of the assets in the energy sector. The asset base of the fund is $1.6 billion.

Investors who prefer to buy individual Russian stocks in any sector can consider the following five companies. These firms trade on the OTC market and were the largest traded depository receipts in 2012 according to a report by BNY Mellon:

1. Company: Gazprom (OGZPY.PK). Current Dividend Yield: 6.28%. Sector: Natural Gas Producers.2. Company: Lukoil (LUKOY.PK). Current Dividend Yield: 5.60%.Sector: Oil & Gas - Integrated.3. Company: Rosneft (OJSCY.OB). Current Dividend Yield: No regular dividends paid. Sector: Oil & Gas - Integrated.4. Company: Norilsk Nickel (NILSY.PK). Current Dividend Yield: 6.84%. Sector: Metal Mining.5. Company: Sberbank (SBRCY.PK). Current Dividend Yield: 1.78%. Sector: Banking".

So, the conclusion is: don't invest in America, invest in Russia instead. By doing so, you strengthen Russian economy and they can invest more in military sector, strengthen their army and get ready for the war. With whom?

And what Russian intelligence (SVR) is going to do about this?

January 12, 2014
I was absolutely right about illegal spy Barack Obama.

Attorney Orly Taitz may have just found a chink in the federal government's armor in protecting Barack Obama from scrutiny, following a judge's ruling over her Freedom of Information Act request from the Social Security Administration (SSA). Taitz has claimed that Obama uses the Social Security number of Harry Bounel and has submitted several Freedom of Information Act requests for the information from the Social Security Administration. Each time, she has been met with stonewalling by the Administration.

Judge Ellen Lipton Hollander has ruled to give Taitz "an opportunity to file a second amended complaint and add allegations of SSA not doing a proper search and withholding records."

Judge Hollander in Maryland gave Attorney Orly Taitz 21 days to file a second amended complaint and add allegations in regards to an improper withholding by the Social Security Administration of records of Harry Bounel, whose Social security number is being illegally used by Barack Obama. When Taitz filed the complaint, SSA did not respond at all. After the law suit was filed, SSA responded by fraudulently claiming that the records were not found. Taitz responded that this is a fraudulent assertion, since the records were found before and denied to another petitioner due to privacy concerns. However, Social Security has no right to claim privacy as according to their own 120 year rule they have a duty to release the records. The judge stated that the plaintiff Taitz might be correct, however at this time she cannot rule in her favor as her original complaint was filed before SSA responded, so the judge gave Taitz an opportunity to refile a second amended complaint and add new allegations, stating the SSA responded but improperly hid the records. This is a great development. This all but assures that the judge will order the SSA to release the SS-5, Social Security application of resident of CT, Harrison (Harry) Bounel, whose CT SSN 042-68-4425 was stolen by Obama and used in Obama's 2009 tax returns, which initially were posted on WhiteHouse.gov without proper redaction, without flattening of the file.

Taitz points out that Andrew Breitbart and Andrew Breitbart and Loretta Fuddy were targeted by Obama for assassination." Breitbart died on the very day that he said he would begin vetting Obama for the 2012 elections, which raised suspicions. Fuddy, best remembered as being instrumental in issuing the Hawaii long-form birth certificate, was the only person to die aboard a small plane that crashed off the coast of Hawaii last week. Already, there are questions surrounding the narrative of her death.

Taitz alleged that Mr. Bounel was born in 1890, and therefore, under the "'120 Year Rule' implemented by the SSA in 2010," pertaining to "'extremely aged individuals,'" Bounel's "Social Security applications have to be released under FOIA without proof of [his] death…"

The reason for the judge's amendment seems to be a procedural one. Taitz filed suit with the court prior to receiving word back from her Freedom of Information Act request, which she did receive on July 29, 2013 from Dawn S. Wiggins, a Freedom of Information Officer. Wiggins replied to Taitz:

"We were unable to find any information for Mr. Bounel based on the information you provided to us. Mr. Bounel may not have applied for a Social Security Number (SSN) or may have given different information on the application for a number".

But once the amendment is submitted, this may force the Social Security Administration to explain exactly what is going on with Barack Obama's Social Security Number.

Obama and Snowden

Obama, Snowden, Putin

June 5, 2013, Hong Kong

Edward Snowden, an American computer specialist, a former CIA employee, and former National Security Agency (NSA) contractor disclosed top secret NSA documents to several media outlets, initiating the NSA leaks, which reveal operational details of a global surveillance apparatus. The release of classified material is called the most significant leak in US history. He revealed such programs as PRISM, XKeyscore and Tempora, as well as the interception of US and European telephone metadata. The reports were based on documents Snowden leaked to The Guardian and The Washington Post. By November 2013, The Guardian had published 1% of the documents, with "the worst yet to come".

Snowden flew to Hong Kong from his home in Hawaii on May 20, 2013, where he later met with journalists Glenn Greenwald and Laura Poitras and released his copies of the NSA documents. After disclosing his identity; he fled Hong Kong and landed at Moscow's Airport on June 23, reportedly for a one-night layover en route to Ecuador. US officials had revoked his passport on June 22. He remained there until August 1, when the Russian government granted him a 1year temporary asylum. Russian president Putin said that if Snowden wanted to be granted asylum in Russia, Snowden would be required to "stop his work aimed at harming our American partners".

Obama pressed Putin very hard to get Snowden back, but Putin refused. Ex-CIA Director Woolsey said that if Snowden was convicted of treason, he should be hanged. One of Snowden's legal advisers, Jesselyn Radack, said that Snowden "has concerns for his safety" based on joking remarks of House Intelligence Committee chairman Mike Rogers about putting Snowden on a "kill list".

One Army intelligence officer offered BuzzFeed a simple plan how to eliminate Snowden: "I think if we had the chance, we would end it very quickly," he said. "Just casually walking on the streets of Moscow, coming back from buying his groceries. Going back to his flat and he is casually poked by a passerby. He thinks nothing of it at the time starts to feel a little woozy and thinks it's a parasite from the local water. He goes home very innocently and next thing you know he dies in the shower."

Why Obama wants Snowden back [or dead -M.K.]?

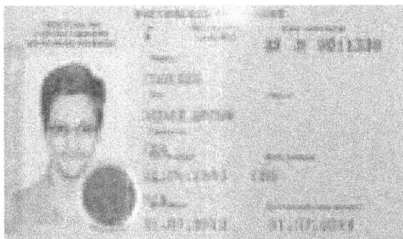

Snowden's Russian refugee ID

Not because of the leaks on NSA activity - it's not a secret at all. Since 1970 NSA is listening to the whole world using the global surveillance Eshelon system.

So, what's Snowden's secret #1 and why Russia is keeping him?

Because he has the NSA documents on Russian Intelligence (SVR) about Obama, Russian spy.

Obama between Rockefellers, Rothchilds and Putin

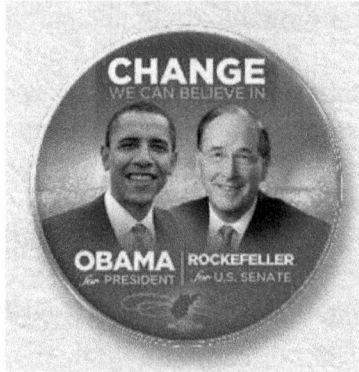

A very interesting 2008 poster: Senator Obama for President and Senator John Rockefeller IV, a great-grandson of John D. Rockefeller, running for re-election.

There are two most rich and powerful families (enemies) in the world - the Rothschilds in Europe and the Rockefellers in USA. They control the world's wealth and financial institutions.

David Rockefeller   Jacob Rothschild

The Rockefeller family is an American industrial, political, and banking family that made one of the world's largest fortunes in the oil business during the late 19th and early 20th centuries, primarily through Standard Oil. The family is also known for its long association with and control of Chase Manhattan Bank. They are considered to be the most powerful family, in the history of the United States. The combined wealth of the family – their total assets and investments plus the individual wealth of its members – has never been known with any precision. John D. Rockefeller was the richest American who ever lived. At the time of his death in 1937, Rockefeller was worth the equivalent of

$340 billion in today's dollars. His company Standard Oil dominated American Oil production and was eventually broken up by The US Government for being a monopoly. Members of the family, especially the banker and statesman David Rockefeller, who is the present family patriarch, have been heavily involved in international politics, and have donated money, established or been involved in the following major international institutions: Council on Foreign Relations, Trilateral Commission, Bilderberg Group, World Economic Forum, Brookings Institution, the United Nations, the United Nations Association.

The Rothschild family established their banking business in the 1760s in Germany.The British branch of the family, was elevated to British nobility at the request of Queen Victoria, being given the two hereditary titles of Baronet and Baron. The Rothschild family is believed to possess the largest fortune in modern world history.

In 2006 N M Rothschild & Sons, an English investment bank, ranked second in UK with deals totaling $104.9 billion. Until 2004, the world price of gold was fixed twice a day, at 10.30 am and 3.00 pm, at the premises of N M Rothschild by the world's main Bullion Houses - Deutsche Bank, HSBC, ScotiaMocatta and Société Générale. Informally, gold fixing provides a recognized rate that is used as a benchmark for pricing the majority of gold products and derivatives throughout the world's markets. Every day at 10.30 and 15.00 local time, five representatives of investment banks meet in a small room at Rothschild's London headquarters on St Swithin's Lane. In the center is the chairperson, who was by tradition appointed by the Rothschild bank. The bank itself has largely withdrawn from the trading which I think is false information.

As for specific members of the modern family, Sir Evelyn De Rothschild the British financier has a net worth of $20 billion, Jacob Rothschild, another British banker, has a net worth of $50 billion. As a modern day an empire, the family's total net worth and assets combined have been pegged in the $300 – $400 billion range.

Both families have their own political "soldiers". Besides, Rockefellers rule Bilderberg Club (through Henry Kissinger), which helps them to rule the world.

And now comes Zbigniew Brzezinski, a former United States National Security Advisor (in 1977-1981, Jimmy Carter administration). Brzhezinski is a Rockefellers' "soldier", for 50 years he was the enemy of the Soviet Union and then Russia. He was secretly meeting Barack Obama in 1981-1983 when Obama was a student at Columbia University. As we remember, before that Obama visited in 1981 India and Pakistan, where he was kidnapped by Russians and changed for a Russian spy. In 2012 Brzhesinski, still a very important person in American politics who serves the Rockefeller family, published a book, "Strategic Vision", where he says that it's OK to be friends with Russia.

So, Rockefellers helped Russian to put Obama on the throne and during his second term at the White House they want to transfer the world power to Russia? They see America is too weak to be a world leader and are ready to "transfer" the power to Vladimir Putin?

Big game, because on May 30, 2012, Rothschild banking clan bought a stake in the Rockefeller group's wealth and asset management business to gain a foothold in the US. The patriarchs of the two families – 96-year-old David Rockefeller and Jacob Rothschild, 76, signed the deal and London-based £2bn RIT Capital investment trust bought a 37 per cent stake in the American's business. In addition to bringing former enemies together, the deal will considerably expand the vast network of both families.

Now Obama has 3 bosses and it looks like at least two of them joined forces for World War III Russian oil and gas? What is his benefit? If the war starts before 2016 presidential elections, he will be re-elected for the third term. The US Constitution doesn't allow it, but that's what happened to President Roosevelt during World War II. And the traditional trick here is – no Communist leader (and Obama is a Communist) left his power for somebody to pick it up else until he's dead of natural causes or killed. Clear?

126

2012

1994

"Bill Clinton has said he would be "happy" if his wife Hillary ran for president in 2016"

April 3, 2012

"It's entirely up to her," Mr. Clinton told ABC News. "I believe that she's being absolutely honest with you when she says she doesn't think she'll go back into politics. But if she comes home and we do this foundation stuff for the rest of our lives, I'll be happy. If she changes her mind and decides to run, I'll be happy." His comments offer a glimmer of hope for supporters of the former first lady, who suggest she would be the best candidate to prevent a Republican claiming the presidency in 2016. After her failed White House bid in 2008, Mrs. Clinton said she held out hope that there would be a female president in the future.

June 20, 2013, Toronto, Canada

Hillary Clinton has fed speculation that she might run for the White House in 2016 by telling an audience in Canada that she would like to see a woman president in the United States in her lifetime.

Many Democrats and Republicans in the United States are expecting her to run, although the 65-year-old Clinton has said she needed to rest after four years as a globe-trotting secretary of state.

Polls have indicated she is far and away the most popular potential Democratic candidate for 2016, and that most Americans would prefer her to several possible Republican contenders. Clinton picked up an endorsement on Tuesday from Missouri Senator Claire McCaskill, who announced she is supporting a group encouraging Clinton to run for the White House. McCaskill, who backed Obama over Clinton in the Democratic primaries in 2008, became the first member of Congress to announce her support for Clinton. She praised the political action committee called Ready for Hillary for using the Internet to build support in the hope that Clinton will run.

In her speech in Toronto Clinton said electing a woman president "would send exactly the right historic signal to girls, women as well as boys and men. And I will certainly vote for the right woman to be president."

October 15, 2013, Atlanta, Georgia

Hillary Clinton may have tipped her hand on Tuesday, October 15, 2013 about her plans for a 2016 presidential run. Speaking in Atlanta at a convention that was closed to the media, Clinton spent 25 minutes talking about the 2011 raid on the Osama bin Laden compound, according to a report in the Atlanta Journal-Constitution. The crux of that discussion: that she was for the 2011 raid in which al Qaida leader bin Laden was killed — and Vice President Joe Biden did not support the military action.

State Representative Tom Taylor, a Republican, told the AJC that Clinton went to great lengths to paint herself and former CIA director Leon Panetta as the raid's fiercest advocates, while at the same time highlighting Biden's opposition.

"Without turning the knife too deeply, she put it to Biden," Taylor told the AJC.

Why take a shot at Biden? Because if Clinton chooses to run for president in 2016, Vice President Biden would likely be her No. 1 opponent in the race for the Democratic nomination, and contrasting her position with Biden's on the bin Laden raid presumably casts her in a more presidential light.

October 20, 2013, Falls Church, Virginia
Hillary Clinton rallied supporters of Virginia Democrat Terry McAuliffe.

Democrats consider Hillary Clinton to be the party's leading contender to succeed President Barack Obama, her onetime rival, if she decides to run for president again in 2016.
When Clinton told the audience that her time traveling the globe had allowed her to think about "what makes our country so great, what kind of leadership is required to keep it great," a man in the audience shouted, "Yours!"

Now Hillary has a huge headache.
As Obama's Secretary of State in 2009-2012 she absolutely supported the Arab spring - a "set" of civil wars and riots in the Arab world that began in December 2010. By December 2013 rulers had been forced from power in Tunisia, Egypt (twice), Libya, and Yemen; civil uprisings have erupted in Bahrain and Syria; major protests have broken out in Algeria, Iraq, Jordan, Kuwait, Morocco, and Sudan; and minor protests have occurred in Mauritania, Oman, Saudi Arabia, Djibouti, Western Sahara, the Palestinian Authority. She was a big advocate of unsuccessful "Bolotnaya" anti-Putin revolution in Russia in December, 2011. She created a very ground for the world war and radical Islamists won't be just observers there. Now, if she wants to be elected the US President, she has to change her position completely and advocate peace. She has to communicate with Putin, whom she

called in 2008 a "KGB agent without soul - by definition". How she can do it? I can help her.

But if she's elected the U.S. President, the peace talks are over. She has to follow Rockefellers' and Rothschilds' orders and start the big war.

January 24, 2014

Priorities USA Action, a non-profit political group which brought in $78 million for Obama's re-election campaign in 2012, confirmed Thursday it plans to raise money for Clinton from rich Democrats. The group named 2012 Obama campaign manager Jim Messina, a veteran political operator with deep ties to wealthy donors, as its co-chair, essentially ensuring the most high-profile Democratic push of the coming election cycle.

January 30, 2014

Hillary Clinton is the Biggest Democratic Presidential Nomination Frontrunner Ever

Hillary Clinton is the biggest frontrunner ever for the Democratic presidential nomination. That's according to a new Washington Post/ABC News poll, which finds former Secretary of State Clinton with a 73-12 lead over Vice President Joe Biden in a hypothetical 2016 Democratic primary race. U.S. Sen. Elizabeth Warren (D-Mass.) gets 8% of the vote. As the WaPo points out, Clinton's 61-point lead is nearly three times as large as it was in 2006, when the conventional wisdom held that she would be the 2008 Democratic nominee. In 2006, she took 39% of the theoretical vote, compared to then-Sens. Barack Obama (D-Ill.) and John Edwards (D-N.C.). But this time, her support is well over 50%.

Army wants Hillary

Obama got a very unpleasant message - American military chiefs don't want to see him in the Oval Office once his 2 constitutional terms are over. He's a Communist and I said before that once Communists get the power they keep it forever and become dictators, supported by the army and special services. The army doesn't want him as Commander-in-Chief when the World War II starts. They love Hillary Clinton

February 9, 2014

Former Army Gen. David Petraeus, who has traditionally stayed away from political endorsements, appears to be eager to support a Hillary Clinton candidacy, a new book alleges.

"She'd make a tremendous President," the former commander and CIA director reportedly says in the new book "HRC: State Secrets and the Rebirth of Hillary Clinton," by Jonathan Allen and Amie Parnes. "Like a lot of great leaders, her most impressive qualities were most visible during tough times," Petraeus adds. Now we know that Hillary Clinton, soon after taking The Secretary of State office, invited Petraeus to her Washington home to drink wine and discuss Middle East issues. The night was so enjoyable that she invited him over again the next night to continue their chat.

Former Gen. David Petraeus shakes hands with then presidential candidate Hillary Clinton in 2008.

Instructions for the White House on top political, military
and espionage management in use by U.S. presidents since
1996

CHAPTER 1
Top Political Management

How to Manage the White House
Be strong. Be attractive. Be logical. *All you have to do during your first term is to take care of the second one.*
The 2nd term's agenda is to set your place in the world's history.
1st year. You have enough public support to start big initiatives.
2nd year. Develop your initiatives.
3rd year. Go, go public preparing your re-election. Presidents often lose voters during this period.
4th year. All-politics year. Try to achieve important international agreement (a treaty) for the historic record. Win re-election.

Divide your day into hours and minutes : 30% of your weekly hours go to senior White House staff, 10% — to Cabinet, 5% — to Congress members, 5% — to foreign leaders.
No matter what, even if it's a war time, sleep one hour during the day to give your brain a break, and finish your day at 6 P.M. After 6 P.M. do not read any documents, do not take any phone calls, do not talk to anybody but family members and close friends. .And - eat whatever you want, but you must know that the more calories you have to digest, the slower you think.

Remember:
1. You are a national image (a national ideal based on pseudo-facts), a symbol of national unity, national continuity and the symbol of federal government. Leadership is the first quality Americans look for in you - they want a President who is steadfast in his convictions.
2. The power to control the federal budget is your top prerogative.
3. Whom are you going to be:
- utopist (ideas manipulator)
- manager (Government and Congress manipulator)
- challenger (reformer)
4. Any problem turns into a political one if it threatens your power.

5. Use your legal right to press the nation and illegal ones to press the world to eliminate problems.

4. Once you're in politics, you are a hostage of your status and you must sacrifice privacy in return for power.

6. Never play alone.

7. All your decisions are risk taking ones (any decision brings a problem). You may ask advice before you make a decision, but don't listen to anybody afterwards. You are not paid for the quantity of your work but for leadership and ultimate decision making.

8. Correct political mistakes fast before they become political scandals.

10. Never blame previous Presidents for the problems they left for you - that's a sign of weakness.

11. Get rid of a White House tradition to deal with problems only if they "knock at the door."

White House Staff

Chief of Staff. The Chief of Staff reviews most of the documents that go to you, gives his advice after intense information processing and consultations with other agencies and then - he's telling others what President wants. A lot of people, including Congressmen and Senators, will try to reach you through him. He has to give good instructions to the Press Secretary on the White House message about current headlines and the President's plans and actions (the Press Secretary works the same way with VP and First Lady press teams).

He is responsible for your time and has to plan at least two months ahead your effective activity together with Communications, Scheduling and other policy offices' Directors plus VP and First Lady Chiefs of Staff. Besides, he has to do "dirty jobs" for the President like firing people or act as a "lighting rod" to draw criticism away from the President.

National Security Adviser. The National Security Adviser controls all the documents concerning national security coming from Defense, State Departments and national security agencies, and coordinates these offices.

His position is not subject to Senate confirmation, which, according to a long-standing Washington tradition, means that he can't be compelled to testify before the Congress. He decides what papers the President should see and, what's more, he gives his comments on any document. (National security is 100% the President's business, so keep this figure at some distance and don't let him think of himself as your Number Two - foreign leaders will try to work through him to get to you or to influence you.) He has to oversee the functioning of the National Security Council (NSC), which is your foreign policy making tool and a "government inside government." This is something very special and convenient about the NSC - it's responsible only to you and there's not much Congress control over its budget. Of course, the National Security Adviser is involved in every meeting between you and any foreign leader and is responsible for the schedule.

The most powerful of executive offices after the National Security Council is the Office of Management and Budget (it's authorized to make cuts in federal agencies' budgets, to advise you on national fiscal and economic policies, supervise execution of the government budget, evaluate the performance of federal programs).

Who they are
Staffers (and Secretaries) prefer stability and don't like it if you're "rocking the boat" - that's why they often play reform-stoppers.

They don't like to work hard and prefer to send you on "very important visits" abroad as often as possible.

They try to load you up with an extremely busy schedule and "feed" you hundreds of useless documents, create artificial problems and conflicts to show off their hyper-activity.

They try to be your decision makers and they do influence you because, unlike Secretaries, they have daily contact with you; that's why you don't see Cabinet members as your principal aides.

They try to set you up by interpreting your decisions and orders in their own way, as every Adviser is the "American President himself."

They know you won't accept "complicated," "expensive," "risky" projects and they try to sell you "simple," "cheap" and "popular" ones only.

Watch your senior staff and how they present ideas. If somebody wants to push his idea or a project, he will give you three options, making two of them unattractive. Naturally you pick the one he presented as least harmful.

Their dirty tricks

1. Fight for access (influence) to President or to people with direct access (aiming to get a better position if President is re-elected).
2. Isolate government from the President.
3. Influence = relationship with the President.
4. Get a table in the West Wing. You are nobody if you are stuck in the White House basement and see the President by appointment only.
5. Before you send a document to the President, have to look at it and ask yourself if it's too immoral or too radical.
6. Never say "no" aloud to anybody.
7. Remain anonymous with conflicts.
8. Never bring bad news to the President - let it be some idiot, not you.
9. Never say "That's impossible," no matter what the President is asking you to do.
10. Disappear (and find an excuse later) if the President is in a bad mood.
11. Never ague with the President if there's somebody else present.
12. Learn how the President likes to do business (talking, giving orders, writing the documents and taking notes, managing official and non-official meetings) and his habits (food, drinks, cigarettes, favorite sport, movies, show business stars, writers, politicians; attitude to women) and try to copy him — the President has to feel comfortable with you.
13. Fight anybody who's trying to do your job to be closer to the President.

14. Avoid taking on risky tasks controlled by the President in person (if necessary, try to "delegate" it to somebody else).
15. Avoid being associated with any failures.
16. Don't say anything President doesn't want to hear.
17. Use "Smith's Principle": if it can be understood by Congress, it's not finished yet.
18. Write memorandums not to inform the reader, but to protect the writer.
19. No matter what subject is under discussion, employ the language of sports and war: say "breakthrough" instead of "progress", never speak of compromise, and consider "adopting a fallback position."
20. Every public appearance in with the President is an investment in your career after the White House.
21. Minimize the number of rivals.
22. Gain independence according to how much the President needs you.
23. Before asking the President for some personal favor, make him believe he's going to get some (political) profit out of it.
24. Tell the President what he can do and help him try to do it, and never tell him what he shouldn't do.
25. Avoid giving any personal gifts to the President if you are not Chief of Staff.

Every public appearance in with the President is an investment in your career after the White House.

There is an open power struggle between national security staff members and domestic policy staff and between those who develop new policies and initiatives versus budget staff.

How to Manage the Staff
Adopt a dominant management style:

1. *Pyramidal*, structured as hierarchy with you at the top, followed by the Chief of Staff and other key assistants. I strongly recommend this one - it insures a clear chain of command and provides precise channels of information going up and directives going down.

2. *Circular*, when you are surrounded by advisers, all of whom have equal access to the Oval Office. That means chaos (JFK style).

All your assistants are political assistants and everyone will try to play a policy-maker. But a good thing is that all of them were not elected and are responsible to you only.

Thus you can:

- reform your staff freely as there's not even a word about it in the US Constitution
- interchange key figures if domestic crisis is approaching
- if you don't agree with the staff on important issues, go to polls for back-up. (The best employee is the one you can blackmail. Besides, a very good "pusher" for your people is their deep understanding that they have to work together to help the President stay in office next term — if the President leaves, everybody leaves)
- use "the carrot and the stick"
- use "pulling by pushing" — give an important job without publicity to those who become too popular
- do as little reading as you can — you have staff for that
- do as little writing as you can — same reason
- involve yourself personally in your staff and Cabinet jobs as little as you can — same reason
- make no minor decisions — same reason
- send back any intelligence or other report if it's more than one sheet of paper

The Cabinet

If the bureaucrats are wearing you down, you have the right to fire any Secretary. However, Cabinet members must be approved by Senate; therefore, you have to negotiate with the Senate leaders and party leaders throughout the country. As a result, some positions may go to people you don't know well and can't trust. Then if you want to re-organize the Cabinet you have to confront the Congress, because Congress tries to protect the interests of its constituents, who are often the clients of the existing bureaucratic agencies. So, if you plan changes you have to appoint people who share your strategy.

You may also need to offer a position to a group that you need to support in the coming election, or whose help you need; or to help pass legislation (these people will be more loyal to their political benefactors than to you).

Secretaries have disadvantages compared to the staffers as they don't have easy access to the Oval Office (again, that depends on you). Some of them had little or no contact with you before being appointed. Actually, their task is to win the backing of key interest groups and that's why you, practically speaking, don't need Cabinet meetings (if there's no crisis). If a Cabinet member feels independent (usually, that's the Secretary of State), don't fire him – substitute him by the national security adviser or send him abroad on a regular basis.

Six positions have Cabinet-level rank, which allows these individuals to attend Cabinet meetings: Vice President, White House Chief of Staff, Administrator of the Environmental Protection Agency, Director of the Office of Management and Budget, Director of the National Drug Control Policy, United States Trade Representative

The Cabinet members work hard during a crisis only. They prefer to save their plans and suggestions for private conversations with you, because that is what you need them for and they are competing with other Secretaries for your time, support and for funds. It's not easy for the President to make government agencies work effectively — first, you have no time, second – they have no competition. Anyway, you must have insiders in all departments, especially in the Justice Department (FBI), CIA and Secret Service firing anybody who's trying to dig dirt on you.

Secretary of Defense. The Secretary of Defense is a very special and unique position for many reasons. This department is regarded a non-political one, defending the United States no matter what (never let him decide, though, what and where US interests are). Military leaders have a lot of friends in Congress who press the administration to accept military demands. Besides, it's not easy to manage the Pentagon, as you depend on the military for evaluations of the national military capacities; they decide also what kinds of weapons to buy and build. Half of the federal budget goes to Pentagon, making it a major department and that's the most frustrating aspect of your management.

You have to find compromise between you, Congress, public opinion, interest groups and defense contractors' lobbyists.

The defense budget affects diplomacy and international relations, because governments worldwide scrutinize it for clues about US global intentions. For example, increases in defense spending, particularly for items such as naval vessels and aircraft, may signal a White House intention to pursue more aggressive foreign policies, and cuts in defense spending may indicate an effort to scale back on defense commitments.

The Cabinet's Hidden Structure

The Cabinet is divided into the inner circle (State, Defense, Treasury, Justice) and outer, less important one (Interior, Agriculture, Commerce, Labor, Health and Human Services, Housing, Transportation, Energy, Education, Veterans Affairs, Homeland Security). While inner Cabinet members are selected more on the basis of personal friendship and loyalty, outer Cabinet members are selected more on the basis of geographical, ethnic or political representation and adopt an advocacy position for their Departments.

The inner Cabinet is divided into two groups:

a) National security group (State and Defense Departments).

b) Legal-economic group (Justice and Treasury Departments).
The Attorney General usually serves as the president's attorney and this special responsibility leads to close personal contact with the President. The Secretary of Treasury is very important in domestic monetary and fiscal policies and international trade and currency.

The outer Cabinet is a "domestic" group. Don't waste your time meeting them - you have enough staffers for that. Sometimes "outer" Secretaries try to build their political base of support within their own bureaucracies. Don't hesitate to fire and replace any of them if they start to criticize you and behave politically independent, counting on bureaucratic and interest groups' support.

There's one (negative for you) thing in common between all Secretaries - self-interest pushes them to protect and expand their departments and then they act more like representatives of their departments to the President then the presidential envoys they were appointed to be ("divided loyalty").

Then Secretaries of State and Defense usually form a coalition against your National Security Adviser. You must be a smart mediator as Commander-in-Chief. These two have weekly meetings, and each of them has a weekly meeting with the DNI (Director of National Intelligence), so you must know from independent sources what they are talking about in case they "forget" to tell you the details. The Defense Secretary meets weekly with the Joint Chiefs, too.

Domestic Propaganda and Mind Control
To effectively manage propaganda you must understand that most political views are acquired through political socialization and the most important influences in this process are the following.

1. Family. If both parents identify with one party, there's strong likelihood that the children will begin their political life with the same party preference.

2. Education. School is a transmitter of patriotism. University is a transmitter of liberalism.

3. Religion. Roman Catholic respondents tend to be more liberal on economic issues than Protestants. Jewish are the most liberal and vote mostly Democratic. Many Northern white Protestants vote Republican, whereas northern white Roman Catholics vote Democratic.

4. Economic status. Poor people vote Democratic. Rich vote Republican.

5. Political events. The war in Iraq divided the nation one-two-three.

6. Influence of opinion leaders. Those are people who have, as part of their job, the task of swaying people's views (politicians and media). Their interest lies in defining the political agenda in such a way that discussions about policy options will take place on their terms.

7. Media. There seems to be no strongly partisan or ideological bias in TV coverage, although the visual and mental images conveyed by TV have a powerful impact.

8. Race. African Americans tend to be more liberal than white on social welfare issues, civil liberties and even foreign policy. They strongly support democrats.

9. Political culture (the set of beliefs and values regarding the political system that are widely shared by the citizens of a nation). Here the most important for us are the degrees of political trust and political tolerance which are measured through a specific series of survey questions, best if done through the Internet.

Mind Control
Every day in 2004 we watched the Homeland Security Department "terror alert colors" and very often the threat was "high" or "very high." With all my 30 years espionage experience I couldn't understand why they were telling the nation about the threat and producing the multicolor picture on TV. Why? What can ordinary Americans do about that? What happened next made the situation absolutely clear for me and posed one more question for the nation: right after President Bush was re-elected the colors disappeared – why? Again, what happened? Is there no more "terror threat" to America? There is. But there's mind control, too. Mind control, which I call mind manipulation or MM, is used to program the "right political behavior" of the nation or "indifferent behavior," if necessary, without people's knowing or understanding the procedure. We are talking here about total illegal social control.

Principles of Mind Manipulation
1) It's not enough if every single citizen, and the nation as a whole, thinks and behaves your way – it's much better if they want to behave your way and feel comfortable, and are absolutely sure it's their own choice and, finally, they become your active supporters.

2) If you want to control the nation and program peoples' thoughts, you have to control knowledge (information, culture and communication).

3) The political imagination (belief) of the nation has to move in the right direction and has to be accepted as the most comfortable and most acceptable way of political activity: nobody is thinking, nobody is criticizing the President, nobody is making comparisons and drawing conclusions. Everybody believes the American President and hates his enemies.

4) Don't waste time fighting foreign ideology, take care of ordinary Americans.

5) There is no difference between commercial and political advertising, and MM.

Propaganda Technology
You need 24/7 effective propaganda to get non-stop public support of your policy — your war for public support doesn't stop the day you enter the White House — it may stop the day you leave the White House. If your polls go below 40%, the United States effectively has no President.
Use the following propaganda tools:
- General (abstract) information on big problem
- Information dosage (the less people know — the easier you convince them)
- Misinformation (full or partial) presented as news, sensations, rumors

- Disorientation – one bit of information contradicts another one
- Provocation – information "pushes" people (before you start war)
- Information over-dosage – too much information (and people lose interest)
- Exaggeration of enemy's negative sides and promotion of scary data
- Distraction of nation's attention from news that is bad (for you) by publishing sensations and (political) scandals
- Stereotype manipulation ("nuclear threat," "international terror," etc.
- "Shuffle" – all news and facts match President's political course
- "Cocktail" – mix of true and false information
- "facts transportation" from abroad (you buy a foreign reporter and he's publishing positive information on your politics; then you spread the information through American media)

Remember the principles of mass psychology: people don't believe the government – they believe the market and the stock exchange; people need statements, not analysis.

Technology of Mind Manipulation (MM)

1) Create a steadfast American collective will-power: "We want to live forever in the America we live in now" - through the media.

2) Don't ask people to change their views and beliefs - they have only to change the object of their aggression - "Now we understand who are America's enemies! (the previous President, Republicans).

3) Get people accustomed to accept facts but believe only in the "right" comments - any common sense has to be "switched off." This way you create *"mass artificial schizophrenia"* — people lose the ability to connect statements and facts (notions) and just believe.

Besides, by extreme exaggeration of the enemy's negative qualities you can install *the national schizophrenic fear* (of "international terrorism") and people have to accept you, the US President, as a savior. Plus, no matter what, repeat your major statements until people start accepting them without thinking.

4) Divide the nation into "good Americans" (patriots) and "bad Americans" (the "minority).
Make it clear: it's much better and more comfortable to be "good" than "bad." "We aren't watching good Americans who support the President. The surveillance is for bad Americans and we make their lives and careers uncomfortable. We have to do that because enemies of America may be using them." This method is called artificial social selection and its ultimate goal is a total regulation and standardization of the nation.

5) For successful MM, use the combined efforts of popular Democratic American writers, TV and radio anchors, talented publicists and columnists, business and show business celebrities, politicians. Thus, step by step you create the "industry of correct political behavior and correct American thinking."

6) Use a combination: statement + image. It reduces the effort needed to understand your message and makes people comfortable with you.

7) Shift all popular TV shows to prime time - Americans don't have to think about politics after they come home.

Psycho-epidemic
During his first presidential campaign Obama used my strategy of psycho-epidemic.
It's simple - you hypnotize people by permanent repetition of a certain word, like "Change!" a phrase, a slogan. A crowd, and even a nation, often behaves like a dog, it's very submissive if there's a strong personality, a strong leader in front of it. Then, the reflex appears - once you see a strong leader, you must listen to him and follow his orders.

Strategic Planning
That's the biggest problem for all administrations. Strategic planning is the process of making present decisions based on very well-calculated future consequences. The basic strategic objective is a decision as to where to concentrate the government efforts — this is the essence of strategic planning.

The worst example of strategic planning is the war in Iraq. It is crucial to choose a professional crew and place people in positions where their brains will work effectively and produce quality.

Planning formula:
- design strategy
- amplify and clarify strategy into policy
- organize a team
- guide execution
- make final strategic decision

A. Regular Planning Model:
Subject, concept, idea definition of objectives
Design of innovative options and debate
Exploration of concepts, claims and possibilities
Development of program outlines
Establishment of expected performance criteria and indications
Information gathering
Integration of ideological elements
Assignment of executive responsibility
Scheduling
Analysis and experiment
Experiment evaluation, examination of likely consequences
Comparison of expected and actual performance levels
Determination of costs
Prognosis
Strategic decision

B. Express planning: information interpretation, projects design, choice of a project, decision

C. Regular (math) model:

Negotiations planning (example): pressure, compromise, tricks, break.

Let's evaluate "pressure": negative international reaction /-1/, breakdown /-1/, positive effect /+1/. Score: -2+1=-1 Conclusion: no pressure should be used.

D. Expertise model.
Government crisis (example): poor planning- wrong decisions- wrong actions- wrong execution- opposition activation- mass protests- coup

E. Scale model.
Risk factors: Risk levels:
International sanctions: medium
High inflation rise: medium to high
High unemployment: medium to high
Low public support level (low polls) : medium

Presidential decision making
1. Decision making is a multiple choice process.
2. Any decision involves political risk.
3. If you can't make a decision, you need more information.
4. Be optimistic, but remain realistic.
5. Give yourself a deadline.
6. No brainstorming chaos.
7. There are two kinds of decisions: irreversible and reversible. Better know which kind you are facing.

Here's the process:
a) Identify the problem
b) Analyze the problem — what are the facts?
c) Evaluate options - what are the pros and cons? What can go wrong?
d) Identify choices - which alternative is the best?
e) Implement plans - what action needs to be taken?

As the world #1 leader you have to know that this world is being ruled not by you but by 11 financial corporations:

Barclays, Goldman Sachs, Capital Group Companies, FMR Corp, AXA, State Street Corp, JP Morgan Chase, Legal & General Group, Vanguard Group, UBS AG, Merrill Lynch & Co Inc.

Bonus
Psychological Modeling of a President
(Strategic Intelligence Method)

Intelligence services worldwide watch political leaders during public appearances, trying to calculate their physical and mental health judging by their look and behavior. In the US they also evaluate the executives and staffers who surround the President at official meetings to calculate what's going on in the White House.
They look at:
- A very detailed biography
- Personal needs, interests, philosophy
- Political views
- Intelligence, will-power, character, abilities
- Behavior in crisis situations
- Compromising facts and possible methods of influence
- Personal, political and big business VIP connections
- Financial situation
- Administration and team
- Political opposition and President
- Congress

Domestic Policy
You can't separate domestic and foreign policies because they are married to the same ugly guy - the budget deficit.

Domestic policy rests on three legs: education, health and environment. Americans will never support reduced funding for education, Social Security and Medicare (Medicaid) cuts and weakened environmental-protection laws. But I strongly advise you – don't bother trying to emulate Europe and the British Commonwealth by providing health care for all – the privately insured middle class (your voting majority) won't stand for it. If you don't believe me, go to the polls.

Now, are you a challenger in politics? If "yes," strengthen your political positions in Washington, DC first, then start some reforms. Before you start a reform you have to win the information war with your opponents and get public support. A reform is always a venture; the process may start taking on momentum and you won't be able to stop it. You had better continue old reforms using a new tactic because new reforms bring new problems, new enemies and new mistakes, and big economic mistakes bring you an economic crises.

Dealing with big business
1. Big organized money moves big political machines, big political machines move big lobbies, big lobbies move the President.

2. The President is an investment.

3. A group that rules the economy rules the White House.

4. A new political course comes not with a new President, but a change of big business' global financial interests.

5. Follow 3 "golden rules":
   - protect big investments
   - help to promote
   - don't interfere

6. If the government doesn't meet the needs of big business, it forms a new one of its own (something like a President's Council). This usually happens when the President can't provide financial stability and super-profits. Besides, big business has much more important foreign connections than the government.

7. Big business is:
a) Money
b) Political and economic control

8. Any political action gets an economic (big business) reaction.

In terms of partisan politics, Republicans are considered to be more sympathetic to big business interests while traditionally Democrats get electoral and financial support from organized labor. Forget about antitrust policy business has become more global and efforts to enforce antitrust policies have proven deficient and are threats to national security.

Managing the Economy

1. Regulate spending, taxation, monetary policy and foreign trade which has to be under strict political control – you have the right to propose legislation and veto any legislation you think incorrect. Keep in mind that Americans always insist on reducing government spending on foreign aid and space exploration, and they naturally hate any rise in taxes.

2. State and local governments, both through national associations like the US Conference of Mayors and Congress Members, always press the government to get more federal funds even at the expense of inflationary budget deficits.

3. Keep unemployment low and prices stable – these two factors are politically dangerous and failure here can bring a free-fall in approval ratings.

4. Take credit for economic growth, price stability and low unemployment even if you have nothing to do with it. Still have problems? Try international initiatives.

There are four inevitable factors that will limit your control over the economy:

i) You must share power with Congress — you can't levy taxes or appropriate money all by yourself;

ii) The theoretical nature of the science of economics — no single economic theory has ever explained the behavior of the economy in the future;

iii) The imprecision of economic information. Economic statistics and indicators do not measure the immediate conditions of the economy, but rather the conditions that prevailed between one and three months ago, depending on the particular economic statistics. Consequently, if you take action on the basis of incoming economic information you may be reacting to a problem that no longer exists or that is much worse than believed.

iv) There are forces outside the reach of the federal government, like international factors (oil prices and foreign trade policies), state and local governments economic decisions and mistakes, big business decisions that affect employment, inflation, the trade deficit and public opinion — which is always against cutting social programs.

Budget Deficit
A large budget deficit is a headache and has extremely negative effects on the economy:
1. It limits the government's flexibility to fight a possible recession; that requires tax cuts and deficit spending, which would exacerbate the debt problem. Since tax revenues fall during a recession and unemployment insurance and welfare payments rise, the budget would be under further strain precisely when deficit spending would be needed to pull the economy up.

2. It reduces the amount of funds available for achieving the nation's social and defense goals, because interest must be paid on the national debt.

3. It can threaten the economy by "crowding out" corporate and private borrowers from the credit market. Because the government must borrow heavily to finance its deficit, it competes with business and individuals to borrow funds. The increased competition forces interest rates higher, causing loans (including mortgages) to become more expensive. As a result, business can afford to purchase less plant and equipment to expand and modernize their operations and fewer consumers can afford to finance purchases of expensive items, such as houses and cars. The resulting reduction in demand threatens economic growth.

4. The US budget deficit has become so large that domestic savings no longer can provide enough capital to service the debt. Consequently, the government must borrow from foreign sources to make up the difference. This makes us dependent on foreign investors and raises the possibility of a "stabilization crisis," which can occur if foreign investors lose confidence in the dollar and liquidate their US investments. Such a crisis could cause the dollar to plummet and interest and inflation to rapidly accelerate.

Crisis
Crisis means that your government as a system is exhausted and it's unable to rule the nation and resources effectively in an extreme situation, including economic, natural catastrophes and war. A crisis has three stages — before the crisis, when the first signs appear; crisis development until culmination; catastrophe followed by impeachment. A crisis could be "programmed" at the very beginning of your term (mistakes in political and economic courses, inexperienced personnel, faulty planning) or it can appear later (too many mistakes, change of political environment, shifts in the economic or international situation). Crisis management includes pre-crisis management and handling of the situation. You must be ready not only for a government crisis but also for sudden military attack, mass riots and natural disasters.

International trade is an important component of national security. Our "friends" (NATO members, Saudi Arabia and Japan) favor a dollar (that is neither overvalued nor undervalued) and a healthy US economy with relatively full employment and low inflation rate. If the dollar is weak, the value of much of their international currency reserves declines and their goods are less competitive in the US market. If the dollar is too strong, their investment capital migrates to the US and the high competitiveness of their products in the US market threatens to provoke calls for trade restrictions. If unemployment in the US rises, the major market for their goods declines. If interest rates are higher in the US than in Europe or Japan, investment capital moves to our country. Consequently, foreign governments press the United States to keep the exchange value of the dollar from fluctuating widely and to hold interest rates steady.

The US Congress Management

1. A Congressional session is a waste of federal time and money — you don't need debates because Congressional staffers can do all the technical work and they can negotiate between themselves and balance positions. Senators and Congressmen don't even have to come to Washington — they can vote from their local offices. So these people can spend their time helping thousands of constituents.

2. The President is dependent on Congressional cooperation to carry out the executive responsibilities of the Office because Congress has to authorize government programs, establish administrative agencies to implement the problems and funds to finance them.

3. It's important if President belongs to the party with a majority in the House and Senate. But if your party loses the majority in Congress, you have to work out new political strategy yourself.

4. President's prestige (popular support or political capital) affects Congressional response to his politics.

5. Influence in Congress is courted only for long periods of service; a Senator with 30 years in office (like Edward Kennedy) has considerably more power than a Senator in his first or second term. This causes the electorate to increasingly favor incumbents, as dislodging one's Congressman or Senator after 30 years, even if the candidate or his party have become unpopular, can be viewed as hurting one's district financially. It is often thought that a freshman would be less able to bring home federal money for his state or district.

6. For most Senators, the Senate is a platform for Presidential election campaign. Senators who openly express presidential

ambitions are better able to gain media exposure and to establish careers as spokespersons for large national constituencies.

7. The first act of a newly elected Representative is to maneuver for election to the Senate. Why? First, they enjoy their position, power and money for six years non-stop. Second, there are only a hundred Senators and the publicity is much, much greater. But Representatives have a much better chance to be re-elected.

8. Congress rejects two thirds of President's proposals.

9. Senators are always looking for a BBD (bigger, better deal) and often shift from one committee to another (a good choice is those dealing with taxes, budget, energy, commerce).

10. Bills to benefit big business move smoothly. (Congress doesn't like the poor — they don't contribute, sorry). To gain majority support for big business legislation members have a special trick — log rolling, when factions combine efforts.

11. Senators don't depend on the people — they depend on the media.

12. If a Senator is blocking the President's proposal, he wants to get the President's attention.

13. When Senators want to bury issues, they create committees.

14. The Senate is a small structure and personal relations between Senators are extremely important.

15. Senators have no incentive to study the details of most pieces of legislation and their decision is simplified by quickly checking how key colleagues have voted or intends to vote.

16.To have power a Senator has to object: much of the Senate work is done by unanimous consent and if you object you'll be approached for sure by some influential people including other

Senators, Secretaries, President's aides or the President himself. They'll try to press blackmail or buy you — and that means you've got a piece of the power pie.

17. Senators avoid responsibility in economic policy.

18. Congress loves the military because military contracts are very lucrative for Congressional districts.

19. Senior Senators teach "newcomers" to vote against any reform which is a threat to their stability.

20. A Senator has real influence on legislation only if he has professional staff in charge of the projects.

21. Senators are afraid to vote against a defense budget increase because then they may be accused of a lack of patriotism.

22. Republicans and Democrats are not really enemies, here, though both sides are always looking for a "traitor" or "insider" in the other camp.

23. The President must have "insiders" in the Senate because the other party could prepare secretly and then launch officially some investigation against you or the members of your Administration.

24. A legislator does exactly what his voters want him to do — stealing federal money from other states and districts, because for him the most important thing is numbers — polls in his state showing how many people approve his activity. His donors watch these numbers too and estimate their investment and the necessity to support re-election.

25. Every member of Congress has a so-called "split personality" — a "Hill style" while working on Capitol Hill and a "home style" while back in the state or district with the voters.

26. A Senator makes a decision only after thinking about what it means in terms of the re-election money that will come to him or to his opponents. His voting decisions depend on his party membership, constituency pressures, state and regional loyalty ideology, interest groups' influence. His stubbornness comes from the fact that he doesn't want to be seen by his constituents as a "rubber stamp" for President's decisions, especially when the bill in question benefits a Senator's state. (And the hidden problem is — you want to move fast, especially during the first year while your personal popularity is high — but for the Congress speed is not important).

27. Sooner or later every member of Congress starts playing the "pork barrel" game. It's nothing else but a diversion of federal funds to projects and places not out of national need but to enhance a member's chances of re-election in his district (military projects, federal buildings, highways construction projects). So be ready for a "Christmas gift" when these fellows add pork barrel amendments to appropriations bills you are about to sign. They often wait until late in each session to pass critical spending bills, which narrows your range of possible responses because a veto may not be feasible if Congress has adjourned and the funds needed to run the federal government are contained in the legislation.

28. In Congress a small percentage of bills (about 500 out of 10,000) actually become law because many bills are introduced merely to get favorable press. The strategy is especially effective if the legislation is "tied" to the headlines of the day (mass murders, natural disasters, ethnic riots etc.).

29. In the Senate it's easier for a minority to block the bill than for a majority to pass it: a 60-vote majority is needed to force a final vote on the bill, while only 41 votes are needed to continue debate and delay a vote.

30. The minority can hold the majority responsible as the party in power for whatever legislation does or does not emerge from the

Senate. But both parties prefer to be the party in power in the Senate - all Senate legislation begins in the committees, whose membership and chairmanship are controlled by the party in power. Besides, each chairman has power in terms of controlling the committee budgets and deciding which hearings will be held and which legislation he will allow to be released to the Senate floor for a vote. He can also "lock up the bill" in committee until it dies. Perfect!

How to Control the Congress

The President can propose legislation, but Congress is not required to pass any of the administration's bills. But you know already that Senators and Representatives need re-election more than anything else. So you can go with indirect influence through appeals to the public; this is a confrontation and direct challenge to Congressional authority. You can also enlist the support of interest groups or direct influence through favors and personal involvement in the legislative process. (Get public support for a proposal before it's discussed with the Congress.)

And don't hesitate to start a national debate — you have enough media attention for that.

You also have an independent tool, presidential power in the form of an executive order. You can give favors directly to members of Congress or to influential people in their constituency, or the favor may be of benefit to the constituency itself:

- Appointments with the President and other high-ranking officials
- Federal grants to recipients in the constituency, government contracts with local companies, the deposit of federal funds in banks, grants to local government and educational institutions
- Support of projects (military installations, research and administrative facilities, public works such as buildings, dams and navigational improvements to rivers and harbors, etc.)
- Recommendations for the US district court judges, attorneys, marshals, etc.

- Campaign assistance (cash contributions from the party's national committee invitations to bill-signing ceremonies, White House parties or to accompany President on trips
- Bargaining and arm-twisting (pressure and threats to lose the projects).

Tools

1. The Congressional Relations Office. Used for:
   - Intense lobbying to form Congressional coalitions if the opposition controls one or both houses
   - Intelligence gathering (of policy preferences — centralized headcounts reveal the voting intentions on a particular bill and constituency concerns of individual members)
   - Representation
   - Creating "inner coalitions"
   - Coordination of executive branch legislative activity (monitoring and tracking bills, controlling departments' staff appointments, collaborating with departments' liaison offices)

Attention! Senators and Congressmen have to trust your people, who must keep their mouths shut; otherwise there will be no business. Anyway, watch these people — a Senator can call one of your assistants and if they hear "no," he will try to reach somebody else until he gets "Yes, the President will see you." Don't let this happen — if it's "no," it has to be everybody's "no." There has to be no difference between personal views of your adviser and your official views.

2. Congressional Relations personnel of various executive Departments are a conduit. Talk to the Secretaries and explain to them that they have to give the Director of Congressional Relations their best people.

3. The White House interest groups liaison staff (office of public liaison)

4. Veto. Threatened with a veto, Senators often seek compromise.

Congress has its ways to undermine your vetoes or threats of vetoes. Because you can't veto parts of a bill, they load up major legislation with amendments on a completely different subject ("riders") that they know the President must accept. (Presidents who vetoed the most bills: Franklin Roosevelt – 635, Harry Truman – 250, Dwight Eisenhower – 181, Ronald Reagan – 78, Gerald Ford – 66).

5. Executive agreement. It permits the President to enter into open or secret agreements with a foreign government without any advice or consent of the Senate. There are two categories of executive agreements:
a) Presidential agreements made solely on the basis of the constitutional authority of the President and under his sole power to faithfully execute the laws (or under his diplomatic or Commander-in-Chief powers). President needs to report secret agreement to the Foreign Relations Committees of the two houses no later than 60 days after such agreement has entered into force. Congress has no authority to disapprove it.
b) congressional-executive agreements, which cover all international agreements entered into under the combined authority of the President and Congress.

Finally, this is what you can do with a bill:
-   sign the bill (the bill becomes a law)
-   do nothing (the bill becomes a law in ten days)
-   veto the bill (the bill does not become a law)
-   pocket veto the bill (hold the bill until Congress is no longer in session, and the bill does not become a law)

Foreign Policy

"Golden rules
1. International treaties have to be negotiated by diplomats prior to endorsement by presidents.

2. The information gathered by spies plays an increasingly role in diplomacy (arms-control treaties would be impossible without the power of reconnaissance satellites and agents to monitor compliance).

3. If you start war, it doesn't mean you failed diplomacy, it means military decision is much more profitable.

4. Make it clear to foreign leaders right away whether you are or you are not going to follow the previous President's foreign policy (after consultations with big business). If you are not going to follow it, design a doctrine of your own (it's a strategy that is the recognized approach or policy of the US government.

5. National security is your top priority and is the "king's job" because actually you have no domestic political obstacles to your foreign policy (if it's a question of war), so you are a chief decision maker there. (The CIA Director has to be excluded from this process — you don't need him. Besides, the CIA even today, no matter how hard I tried to educate the Agency, remains the worst of the worst and is not to be reformed — it has to be abolished. We have to transfer political intelligence functions to Pentagon. National security is designed to protect the United States and the vital interests (investments) of big business and to promote American values in a world of rivals, and the CIA, through all 60 years of its history, has proved to be absolutely unsuitable for the job).

6. Any country has to be involved in the sphere of our strategic interests if it has a strategic geographic position, significant sources of raw materials, a well-developed transportation system, or could be used as a military base. The strategic policy of any country rotates around the USA and if not — that means a certain President is waiting for greater incentives to come on board. Against target countries, don't hesitate to use the strategies of pre-emptive war, post-war (post-crisis) reconstruction, and nation building (which means erasing national identity and supplanting it by liberal values).

With China's growth, the Cold War is back with a vengeance, so we are back to secret deals based on spheres of influence — but that's a temporary strategy.

7. You can't always do what you want without help - you are dependent on other world leaders, Congressional positions and international public opinion. Ask the Senate to help you sometimes - believe me, they'll be happy and proud to do so.

8. Create super-profitable conditions for big business by political penetration worldwide. Big money men start investing abroad when they find a safe environment — law and order. The more they invest the more political power they get (international corporations is the most important element of international system; the other two are governments and non-governmental organizations).

9. Use big investors to ruin other national economies and governments by withdrawing finances when the economic situation is worsening. As soon as the country opens its financial markets, it increases its dependence on global economic processes that it cannot control; and a financial crisis can easily be staged. Conversely, other countries' access to the US markets is a powerful economic and political tool.

10. Make the US markets the most attractive for investors by provoking unstable situations in other countries and regions.

11. Send troops or work through military intelligence (not the CIA) to wherever you perceive a threat to the US investments.

12. Use pressure everywhere — strategic nuclear missiles are still the most powerful blackmail tool. Remember, if you are dealing with Russia or China, they will look not only for agreement, but for advantages.

13. Use "personal diplomacy" — phone calls to foreign leaders (every planned phone call has to go through the National Security

Adviser and be well prepared, like a serious negotiation). Most important are phone calls to our allies — NATO members. Don't forget to wish happy birthday to the leaders in person!

14. Use "informal diplomacy" – recruit politicians in other nations who might be able to give informal access to a country's leadership. In some situations, such as between USA and China diplomacy is done through semi-formal channels using interlocutors such as academic members or think tanks. This occurs in situations when presidents wish to express intentions or to suggest methods of resolving a diplomatic situation, but do not wish to express a formal position.

15. Don't hesitate to use summits as a tool, because:
- if you meet a foreign leader in person, you can reduce tensions and clarify national interests.
- personal relationship may lead to improved relations between nations.
- summits allow you to focus national attention on specific issues.
- presidents engaging in personal diplomacy are much more capable than career diplomatic bureaucrats of understanding the domestic policy consequences of diplomatic actions.
- summit negotiations can yield quick results, since discussions are between leaders with the power of decision rather than between representatives who must receive instructions, make reports and rely new proposals.
- diplomatic impasses may be overcome at summits by shifts in policy that only top leaders are empowered to make.
- if presidents desire an international forum for their diplomatic policies, a summit meeting can provide one.
- successful summits can enhance the image of the President and the United States

16. If you're ready to fight for national interests, forget about human rights — you can always blame infractions on the other side.

17. Isolation is the greatest enemy to information.

18. There's no sense in applying sanctions if big business isn't interested.

19. Economic and hence, political progress for any country affects the USA through economic competition that threatens the market and jobs.

20. Any initiative is risky if it's about unstable region, but you lose popularity fast if you are perceived as indecisive or weak in foreign policy.

21. Any trip abroad has to convey a strong message.

22. Direct military intrusion indicates weakness in your foreign policy. If it's inescapable, involve as many allies as you can.

23. Don't touch our military bases abroad!

24. Big debts open markets. No matter what, open national markets world-wide for American big business and remember - the markets, not Presidents, rule the world.

25. Tie your allies to international economic projects and make them pay most of the expenses.

26. Never talk about money in public — talk about democracy, human rights, liberal values and disarmament — people like it.

27. Move forward — transform Americans' national and patriotic feelings into nationalistic ones (follow the French model) to get total support of your policy (see "Mind Control").

28. Don't pay too much attention to the CIA - all they have to do is to support you with appropriate information to justify your strategic political decisions - and nothing else.

29. Ignore the UN - Secretary General has no real power, but you can take advantage of such a thing as the UN peace-keeping if it corresponds with your interests - the US economic costs could be minimized. Besides, UN peacekeeping can promote a spirit of international accountability in solving a certain regional problem. Don't forget to explain your strategy to the Congress - they don't like the UN either. On the other hand, you have to manage an international crisis, if it threatens our national interests (start with strategic planning, check national security system for the adequate response, use propaganda to get domestic and international support, consult with big business and allies, start crisis negotiations if possible, use diplomacy (see below) and force or threat of force).

30. To reach global leadership you must have enough resources, national support and a well-calculated strategy (see also "Strategic planning"). As you already know, the US budget is financed by foreign lending. When the dollar goes down in foreign exchange markets, it's supported by foreign central banks and you're OK as long as Japan, Saudi Arabia and Germany have an interest in propping up the American economy and do not raise the price for financing America's debt. The worst situation would be to lose support both at home and abroad

Foreign policy decision making:
- assessment of the international and domestic political environment
- goal setting. We have multiple foreign policy goals, and we must determine which goal is effected by the international and domestic political environment
- determination of policy options
- decision making action
- implementation of chosen policy option

World Domination
Securing the top position requires:
- economic domination
- military power — pre-emptive war or blackmail by war (seeking domination requires an inevitable increase in the military budget)
- a cultural and media invasion
- special operations to influence or neutralize leaders with negative attitude.

Modern mechanism of world domination
1. If the country does not accept American rules of the game, we start a "velvet" or "colored revolution.

2. We replace the government by pro-American regime.

3. If the government resists, we start the US and NATO military operation and help the anti-government organizations to overthrow the government.

Strategies used
1. Destabilization strategy based on terrorism - you kill political leaders and civil population, blow up government buildings and blame the opposition.
2. Stabilization strategy - first, "terrorists" destabilize the situation in the country and then the US and NATO troops come to "stabilize' it.
3. "New order" or a "managed chaos" strategy - American "new world order" through the international chaos, permanent wars, civil wars and revolutions.

My definition : *"Managed chaos" strategy - geopolitical re-division of the world by provoking riots, revolutions, civil wars and overthrowing regimes in independent from USA sovereign states to keep the U.S. world hegemony. Political, national, religious and social conflicts in target countries have to be permanent. The strategy is being covered by a "struggle against international terrorism". The operation is preceded by information war against the target regime and backed by NATO forces if necessary (Lybia).*

Most important targets of the 21st century – Russia and China. That's the reason we occupy Afghanistan and have to circle China with our military bases in Central Asia.

4. Global energy control strategy - the US control of major oil regions and gas fields.

To keep America on top, we would have to prevent cooperation and coalitions between: China and Africa; Shi'ia and Sunni Muslims; Germany and France; Venezuela and Cuba. Their trade agreements and alliances will change the geopolitical situation.

In most important world regions keep the balance by supporting the country which follows the leader:

In Europe — support Britain to balance Germany. You rule Europe if you rule the Persian Gulf. You rule the world if you rule Europe, and that's why you have to keep NATO by all means to block the military independence of Europe (Germany).

In East Asia - support Japan, Russia and Taiwan to balance China.

In South Asia support Pakistan to balance India.

In Latin America — support Argentina to balance Brazil.

Diplomacy

1. Use secret visits (send the National Security Adviser) if the international problem is complex and important — in this way you don't depend on media and public opinion. Afterwards you can talk, if it was a success.

2. If presidents like to drink with each other, they are ready to deal with each other.

3. Avoid negotiating on major issues at the end of the day, when your energy is low.

4. Negotiate smart, watch your initiatives. The more you tell about your position, the less your partner will tell you about

himself and the higher price you'll pay. Diplomacy is all about money and the essence of any negotiations is the price range.

5. Any information should be exchanged as a part of a compromise and not merely given away.

6. Always talk less than necessary. Concentrate on facts and never tell other person about feelings (or your family and medical problems). Don't interrupt others; try to understand what they really want and if they try to manipulate you. Also, resist giving in to interruptions until you have completed your thoughts – "Just a moment, I haven't finished". Use Taleyran approximation – if it's difficult for you to speak up, try to make just one diplomatic statement. If they press you, insist on moving these questions to experts. And use indirect language such as "It looks like" or "You see situation from a very special angle".

7. No negative emotions - strong emotions indicate weak nerves. Realize that there might be other issues motivating the other person's behavior and never take things personally.

8. Stop self-limiting behaviors, such as smiling too much, nodding too much, tilting your head or dropping your eyes in response to other person's gaze. Speak I normal conversational volume, don't scream and don't whisper, either, as you won't be taken seriously.

9. Take a problem-solving approach to conflict, and try to see the other person as your collaborator rather than your opposition. You'd better postpone negotiations than allow them to break down.

10. Fix all questions and don't be in a rush to answer any of them.

11. The slower you talk, the more confident you are.

12. Never ask straight questions.

13. It is important to know what questions and when you have to ask. Start with an "invitation" question that does not need a definite answer but opens up the discussion, like: "No matter what reporters say, we'll start negotiating for arms control." Proceed with "intelligence gathering" questions, like: "Are you going to abide by our last agreement on the withdrawal of military forces or do we have other options?" Go to "expertise" questions, like: "It's 5000 soldiers, right?"

There's a difference between expertise and straight questions - straight question are like: "Will you sign the treaty?" and these have to be avoided because you'll get no straight answer right away. Finish with a closing question, like: "I think that's what we intend to sign? Next time we can start from here." Or you can press your partner: "Let's not lose this last opportunity, eh?"

14. Explain your negative attitude in a smart way: give half the information and continue, depending on your partner's reaction. If you can't accept his proposal, tell him that the experts may look into it again and come to agreement. If your partner is not a complete idiot he'll understand his proposal is unacceptable (because the experts have already done all they could). But if he is an idiot, he'll agree to "kill" his proposals by passing them to the experts.
You start to lose momentum if you start to defend yourself.

15. Stop (postpone) negotiations the moment you start to lose or you could end up in a total failure and that could be used by opposition back home.

16. If you bring ideology - try to win. If you bring national interests, try to find compromise. Be flexible — that's a sign of strength, not weakness.

17. Don't make aggressive statements for the media, no matter what.

18. Respect is half a victory, but you usually win when your partner is scared. Avoid open confrontation and respond to personal attacks with humor.

19. Watch the military experts - they are always ready to "push" you. No arms agreement can win ratification without backing from Joint Chiefs, because Congress needs and trusts their expertise, and their disapproval is a strong tool against you in case you ignore their advice. So, think three times before you appoint Joint Chiefs.

20. Take negotiations on the trade deficit very seriously — they often take you nowhere and have zero results as your partner wants you to change your attitude to him completely as well as your international economic policy, while you expect the same favor from him. You can influence one partner but you can't very easily influence the international system.

21. After you come back home do some positive advertising through the media — in such a way you influence other presidents and future negotiations. If the negotiations resulted in a treaty, "sell" it to the Senate for approval.

22. Negotiation no-nos:
    - don't be confused if your partner threatens you — that means he needs your cooperation. Don't enter into negotiation right away with high demands.
    - don't touch the toughest issues first. Don't assume — that's a sign of weakness.
    - don't hesitate to pause or take a break.
    - never say "no" to your partner's ideas — rather, pack them up in one "package" with your proposals.

Diplomatic tricks.
Tricks in diplomacy are usually used to distract your hard working team, shift the emphasis of the negotiation in order to shape the deal on terms of your adversary or manipulate your

team into closing negotiation and accept terms you don't really like. And the tricks are:

"Leap" - your adversary is losing and starts "jumping" from one point to another

"Pile" - your adversary "piles up" problems, tries to provoke a chaotic discussion or stop negotiations

"Empty chair" - a day or two before negotiations start your adversary informs you that he's not ready yet, trying to press you (or he wants to change location)

"Diplomatic illness" – the practice of feigning illness to avoid participation in negotiations and at the same time to avoid giving formal offense.

"Deaf" - your adversary keeps asking questions instead of answering yours

"Provocation" — your adversary doubts your team's professional level and your ability to negotiate

"Busy guy" — your adversary breaks negotiation for an hour or two pretending he has to do some very important business (or that he got a very important call).

"Mirror" - it's a very interesting "programming" trick. The technology is simple: you try to "mirror" your adversary's style and behavior, adopt a similar posture, use his gestures, and follow the speed of his speech. First, he will like it subconsciously and will be more open to you. Second, you'll understand better his way of thinking.

"Sandwich" - pressure (often — military) — negotiations — pressure

"Show" - using certain arguments your adversary appeals to your emotions

"Circle" - a very sophisticated trick: your adversary tries to "push" his proposal in different variants and finally comes back to his initial variant, trying to convince you that's the best choice

"Carrot and stick" - threat (blackmail) plus promises (money). The guy could blackmail you also by demanding to set a deadline

"Student" - your adversary talks too much about the details, asking a lot of minor questions, trying to make you nervous and make mistakes

"Donkey" – your adversary declines the offer to speak first

"Ball" - encourage your adversary if he's looking for "global decisions" and he'll do a lot of minor favors

"Rubber" - delay, if you can't predict the result, and press your adversary by delaying the answer

"Last train" - you can press your adversary by an ultimatum right before negotiations are over, if he really is interested in some result. "Spice" the ultimatum with some important reasons and give your adversary a choice of variants.

You can also leak opposing demands to the media (be careful with this one. Do not betray diplomatic trust by talking about secret deals or demands that actually have been mentioned). You may also escalate your demands during negotiation and manipulate public opinion to line up behind your demands.

Negotiations Procedure
I. Preparation
1. Write a plan.

2. Define your objectives.

3. Identify issues that are open to compromise and those that are not.

4. Conduct research for information to support your objectives and have information to undermine your partner's position; think what information is available to your partner (State and Defense Departments will help you with that; not the CIA).

5. Find out how your partner negotiates with other leaders (he might have a "rabbit in a hat" for you).

6. Consult with members of a previous negotiating team about his style, strong and weak points.

7. Check the current balance of power. Attention: if you start multilateral negotiation you have to know what are the conflicts or allegiances between other partners. If they are divided into groups, identify who has the power to make a decision on behalf of a group.

8. Use game theory if you are intending to cooperate. Game theory is a theoretical analysis of the decision-making process taken by two or more players who are in conflict. You must actually estimate any possible strategies of the players who have to make decisions without knowledge of what other players are planning. Each player's strategy, once undertaken, will affect the others. Game theory is often illustrated by the "prisoners dilemma" paradigm. It supposes that two men have been arrested on a suspicion of committing a crime together and are being held in separate cells. There is not enough evidence to prosecute unless one confesses and implicates the other. Both of them know this but cannot talk to each other. The dilemma is that the best outcome, not being convicted, is only available if they each trust the other not to implicate him. If X decides to trust Y, but Y fears X may not be trustworthy, Y may confess to get a lesser sentence; X then gets a worse one. The best solution to this dilemma is for both to cooperate, to minimize the worst that can happen, rather than trying for the outcome that is maximum. This is called the minimax strategy and it's classified as being the most probable outcome.

II. Conducting negotiations
Never conduct negotiations before 10 a.m. or after 4 p.m.
First of all, you have to decide whether you want to speak first or to respond to your partner's proposal. There's an advantage in letting your partner make the opening proposal as it might be much more beneficial for you than you suspect.
Then:

a) Put forward a proposal (with as little emotion as possible). You have to make your initial offer-demand high and compromise from that point onward. Your partner will understand perfectly well it's too much, so make your initial demand greater than you expect to receive, and offer less than you are expected to give. (For the same reason feel free to reject the first proposal received.) While talking further, leave yourself room for maneuvering, presenting your proposals, and don't try to pin down your partner to a fixed position too soon, because he needs room to maneuver, too. Make a final offer when the atmosphere is most cooperative.

b) Respond to proposals in a smart way (again, no emotions). Never take the first offer – if you take it, your adversary may feel there is something wrong with it or he didn't get the best deal. Capture any similarities on both sides. Don't hesitate to make conditional counter-offers: "If you do this, we'll do that." Cut the unexpected introduction of new issues and follow strictly a concise step-by-step agenda. Probe your partner's attitudes: "What would you say if we both lower our demands?" but indicate that every concession you make is a major loss to you. Ask as many questions as you want — the more information you have, the more you control negotiation. To think over and re-design your strategy, ask for a break as many times as it's acceptable. Summarize your partner's proposals.

c) Move towards a bargain. You must know perfectly well the response to each of your points before you open your mouth. If your aides can't help you, you have the wrong aides and you even might be a wrong president. Offer the lowest price first, as you may not need to go any further. Negotiate a "package," don't concentrate on one demand and link other, smaller demands to it. While making a final offer look at the other party and check the body language (see below), your team members must confirm by body language that this is your final offer. It's OK to press the partner by emphasizing the need to reach agreement, like: "We know our nations are waiting to see the treaty signed." (If your partner looks at his watch, it means he wants to end the talk.) If you see you are approaching a dead end, ask your partner to talk off the record, in private, but if you talk in private, you have to keep your word no matter what.

Sometimes negotiations (as in the Israel-Palestine case) run into serious problems and breakdowns. Strong diplomats never say "never" and never leave forever, and always are ready to come back and agree right away on new dates to continue talks, as though a breakdown is just one more pressure trick. The best thing to do is to re-establish communications as soon as possible and you have to do this through your team member who has good connections and influence with other party. Act fast, especially if the consequences of "no deal" would be worse than the last deal that was on the table. If the situation is not improving, you have nothing else but to use a mediator. I do not recommend you to take responsibility as mediator or to use a mediator for your diplomatic needs. International experience shows that these old and "experienced" people usually make the situation worse, like bringing in a lawyer — even if the situation looks better for the next couple of years. But if you have no choice and your partner, and your aides insist on using a mediator to resolve the situation you have to think it over ... and agree.

Mediation is the process in which deadlocked parties consider the suggestions of a third party, agreed upon in advance, but are not bound to accept the mediator's recommendations. The mediator works as a referee between the negotiating parties and tries to find common ground among their agendas. Once some common ground is established, the mediator can begin to look for mutually acceptable ways out of the deadlock. A mediator between presidents has to be a president himself, very influential, and well informed on the situation to be able to make effective recommendations.

He has to:
a) consider the situation from all angles
b) help both parties to understand each other better
c) help the parties to create new approaches
d) suggest a solution, give alternatives

But if the two sides' demands are too far apart, no outside party can bring them together at all. (Often a mediator has to make multiple trips between two parties, who do not talk directly, and it's called shuttle diplomacy. Usually, two parties do not formally recognize each other, but still want to negotiate. The term became widespread following Henry Kissinger's term as National Security Adviser and then, as the United States Secretary of State (in 1973-1977), when he participated in shuttle diplomacy in the Middle East and China).

III. Closing negotiation

That's the most important part, a final mutual agreement or disagreement, a test for your foreign policy making strategy and tactics and personally for you, your power and your image. Any treaty you sign with foreign leaders, if it meets American interests, is not your personal success, but that of the nation. There are three options:

a) the agreement with all conditions is acceptable to both parties
b) the agreement is acceptable to one party only
c) the agreement is unacceptable for both parties

Diplomatic Double Talk
Statement
We are disappointed.

Meaning:
We got nothing.

Situation disturbs us.
Meaning: It's unacceptable no matter what.

There are still differences between our approaches to the problem.
Meaning: There are huge differences.

We can't accept this deal.
Meaning : This means trouble.

We reserve the right to use any means to prevent further worsening of the situation.
Meaning: This means war.

Discussion helped us to understand each other better.
Meaning: We've wasted our time.

We don't understand your attitude.
Meaning: Stop it immediately.

I'm trying to understand your position.
Meaning: Understand me too, idiot!

If I've understood you correctly, you don't agree.
Meaning: Do you have any other option?

We both will pay a very high price if we don't reach agreement.
Meaning: Yes, that's a threat !

CHAPTER 2
Espionage Management

Spy Code

1. No mercy, no ideology, no emotions.

2. Intuition is nothing but the ability to watch and analyze.

3. No evidence is evidence in itself.

4. Distrust is a mother of security.

5. Never look as if you are sizing up the person — that's a sign that gives away cops and spies.

6. Don't start first if you don't know the rules.

7. The way you act is the way you think — behavior is a system of codes (information) which could be calculated by the enemy. Watch your face — that's a shop window.

8. Think fast, talk slow.

9. Avoid self-programming and never think bad about yourself.
10. Don't smoke, drink or take drugs if it's not necessary; spare your stomach from very hot or cold food or drinks; avoid too much noise and light.

11. Don't be shy to lie — the more you lie the more people respect you.

12. Let people talk out and "empty their brains" — then load your information.

13. People never change — everybody wants to get pleasure and avoid pain.

14. "He knew too much" means "He talked too much."

15. Never ask extra questions — wait. Wait and the object will get used to you and open himself — nobody can stay tense for long.

16. Lonely people live longer in espionage business.

17. "No exit" situation is the one you don't like or don't understand.

18. Avoid:
   - personal enemies (they fix negative information on you)
   - silent types (they notice and think too much)
   - other professionals (they'll blow your identity)
   - extra stress (it damages your heart and blood vessels and that kills your brain and your ability to think)
   - talking too much

19. The best weapon against your enemy is his enemy.

20. "I want nothing" means "I want everything".

How to run agents (secret sources)
You can get tons of information through technical devices but no device can influence decisions made by leaders of other countries. That's why for thousands of years to come, a reliable agent will be the top tool of any special service, and their actual names have to be kept secret forever, please. A VIP agent (a top government employee) is a very rare thing and depends hugely on luck, because he can make or influence big political decisions. If he has access to the Oval Office, he can change the President's plans and strategy, and can sabotage political, economic or military actions. When major presidential initiatives fail, time after time, one might wonder who is sabotaging whom.

The most important thing a secret source can get is reliable information on any possible attempt on the US President's life, or concerning a decision of a foreign government to start a war against the United States. A professional agent is actually is both an instrument (to get information) and a weapon (to influence or neutralize people).

Categories:
A. "Garbage" (60%), the "no trust" category.
Recruitment is #1 priority for the officer and a part of his working plan and very often he has to recruit people who are not born agents. You can work with a nice guy, teach him, pay him, press him — and he still avoids any cooperation (busy, sick, on vacation, etc.). It's hard to get rid of him because, first, you have to explain to your superiors why you recruited garbage and second, there's a rule: if you want to be very smart and innovative, a reformer, who came here to start intelligence revolution and get rid of a passive agent, recruit an active one first. Also, agents who work under pressure (blackmail) sooner or later slide into this category.

B. Good agents (30%), middle category. They adhere to the rules of discipline and keep the schedule (that's very important even if there's no information), deliver a lot of information that you have to verify through other sources, but don't show much initiative. Used for regular espionage: go and talk to the object, copy documents, make a recording, take pictures, listen, watch. You can trust them and check often, anyway.

C. Born agents (10%). You are very lucky if you can recruit such people. They betray their country with pleasure and sometimes do not even ask for money because it's in their character — they are looking for adventure or are not happy with their personal or professional life and seek improvement or revenge. They take risks, have good analytical abilities, good education, make (VIP) connections easily, "crack" any object, play the "good guy" whom you can trust. Sometimes they come to you as volunteers, and if they bring valuable stuff — recruit them

D. Women. Women are a special category here, as elsewhere, and the rule is: if you can't recruit a real agent, you recruit a woman. It's not professional to recruit a woman for a serious operation, but if you want to get to an important object, a woman can introduce you. OK, you can recruit a US Senator's secretary or a typist from the Pentagon, but it will be on your conscience if she gets caught. Such cases entail a life sentence; usually — how would you feel? Besides, women often fall in love with their objects and tell them everything. Finally, a married woman is much bigger problem than a married man.

Recruitment
Recruit a small number of well-informed people. Do not recruit:
- psychos
- volunteers (unless it's a "mole" or other government employee who brings you top secret information right away. In a counter-intelligence set-up, a "volunteer" will try to get information about you, telling the minimum about himself.)
- persons with low educational and intellectual level
- people under 30 or over 70, unless it's a VIP. (Did someone get Jim Baker? Dick Cheney?)
- mafia members
- people who are happy with their lives and careers

The best formula when you recruit is a mix of money and ideology (brainwashing). It's not necessary to sign recruitment obligations — people take that as a blackmail tool. It's enough if the fellow brings a good piece of information and get paid (make a video, anyway).

Recruitment Pyramid
Priority recruitment candidates in the USA:
President
The White House staff
The Cabinet and federal agencies
The US Congress
Big corporations
Big scientific institutions

Local politicians
VIP world (celebrities — big media, show biz, big sport)

Candidates for recruitment

1. All spies who work in the USA under legal "cover" as diplomats, reporters, scientists, businessmen, actors, artists, musicians, sportsmen have the legal right to make and develop any contacts and invite people to private parties; then they "transfer" these contacts to professional recruiters. Any embassy can invite any politician to official and private parties and "work" with him there. Besides, all those people can invite prospective candidates to their countries or to other country to develop the contact; it's much easier to recruit abroad. And remember, any contact, any talk, any piece of biography is already information.

2. You can get information about candidates through other agents and through the media.

3. It's useful to install listening devices in the government buildings or listen to the phones, and collect compromising information on politicians. I recommend listening to the phones all over the city, if it's the capital of the country.

"Golden" rules

1. Do not tell the agent about problems and mistakes of the agency, about your personal problems, about other agents, about his own file and compromising information you have on him.

2. Don't show him any classified documents — you might provoke him to sell the information to somebody else.

3. Don't trust your agents too much; they can use you to compromise their personal enemies.

4. Never criticize the source — be an adviser. Don't talk straight if he avoids cooperation or brings you garbage — just reduce or stop payments, or get rid of him.

5. You lose the agent if you don't pay him for a job well done, ask him to "produce" fake information (to show your bosses how much great espionage activity you have going on) or if you don't care about his personal security and his personal problems (health, career). And — never give poison to your agent for security reasons.

Questioning the source
This is of extreme importance — the right question brings you the right answer and top secret info. Give your agent a chance to tell and show you everything he's brought, no matter how chaotic the story might be or how ordinary the documents look. Don't make written notices. Don't bring written questions even if you are talking about some advanced technology — look and be professional. Don't let the agent analyze the information before he talks to you and don't let him bring it in a written form — it's usually not complete; he can lose it; or it may be stolen from him. If there are documents, he has to bring a microfilm. Ask questions — When? Where? What happened? Why? What's going to happen next?

After that you tell the story back to him and he adds details. At the end of the meeting give the agent another task and don't ask him to bring you "something," because he'll bring you just that "something" and nothing else.

Remember, questioning is not interrogation; do not bring another officer to the meeting because it will look like cross interrogation.

Teaching the source
Teach your agent to:
- follow security rules while talking to people, working with the documents and especially meeting the officer (some foreign agencies practice open contacts with many people, hoping that the meeting with the agent won't attract much attention — I don't recommend that)
- always stay calm in stressful situations
- always keep discipline and come in time

- use analytic abilities working with people and documents — ask yourself as many questions as you can

Checking the source

You can never be sure you are not working with a "double agent," even if he brings you top secret stuff. Besides, agents are human beings and they make mistakes — they forget about security, spend too much money, talk too much and ask extra questions; if arrested they may not play the hero but will tell everything. Anyway, you can check your source:

a. by fake arrest followed by severe interrogation.

b. through provocation (tell him you know about his "double game" and watch his behavior after the meeting (it's good to have a listening device or a camera in his house).

c. by making an analysis of all the information and documents he delivers and comparing it with information from other sources.

d. through other agents.

e. through your "mole" in counter-intelligence (if you're lucky).

f. through technical devices (reading the mail, listening to the phone, secret searching his house and office, watching him through hidden cameras, trying surveillance in the street).

Agent termination (one-way ticket)

It doesn't happen often but you have to know some special situations when you have to terminate the agent:

1. He knows too much (talks too much) and is ready to betray you.

2. VIP agent (politician) is under suspicion and you can't help him for political reasons (diplomatic, international scandal, etc.)

— in such a case an accident could be staged. It happens that the agent is too close to President.

3. Agent was involved in special operations (murders) and is dangerous as a witness.

4. Agent is trying to blackmail you.

5. You need to press (blackmail) other agents.

Special Influence
1. Tortures
Torture is a category of methods of interrogation designed to shock, hurt and humiliate the object and get information or to make him do something (if used for blackmail). Points to remember:
- ongoing torture decreases pain sensitivity
- people with strong will power take torture as a test
- resistance to torture is often a form of hysterics after arrest
- the object could take himself as a martyr if you torture him too much
- torture could damage object's psyche and you won't be able to work with him (that's why we keep terrorists in Guantanamo Bay without trial – we turn them into idiots)
- people usually trust "after torture information" more than voluntary confessions
- there are different types of torture and professionals often combine them

Techniques of psychological torture include:
- fake execution
- complete isolation ("wall therapy")
- daylight deprivation
- forcible narcotics addiction. Here you can use depressants, stimulants, opiates or hallucinogens: depressants (alcohol, barbiturates, antianxiety drugs with

effects of euphoria, tension reduction, , muscle relaxation, drowsiness; stimulants (cocaine, amphetamine, methamphetamine (crystal meth), with effects of fast euphoria, exhilaration, high physical and mental energy, reduced appetite, perceptions of power , and sociability; hallucinogens with effects of euphoria, hallucinations, distorted perceptions and sensations

- making the object observe others being tortured (such as family members)
- abuse of object's national, religious feelings or political views)
- The effects of psychological torture are: anxiety, depression, fear, psychosis, difficulty concentrating, communication disabilities, insomnia, impaired memory, headaches, hallucinations, sexual disturbances, destruction of self-image, inability to socialize
- Techniques of physical torture include:
- food, water, sleep deprivation
- damage to vital body organs (brain, lungs, kidneys, liver, private parts) plus electric shock. The brain is particularly dependent on a continuous and stable supply of oxygen and glucose.
- rape
- face deformation
- water cure (the torturer pours water down the throat of the subject to inflict the terror of drowning. In another variation, the subject is tied or held don in a chair, his face is covered with a cloth or plastic sheet, and water is poured slowly or quickly over his face to encourage him to talk

The effects of physical torture are: extreme (unbearable) pain, hypertension, fatigue, cardiopulmonary and other disorders, brain atrophy.

2. Special psychology
I. "Brain washing" (implantation of new ideas). The process is: isolation from outside world ("information vacuum") — sleep and food limitation (very effective) — "bombing" with slogans –

ideological aggression – achieving the result (brain is loaded). The object is now ready to brainwash newcomers.

II. "Behavior modification" (by placing into a group). The process is: initial contact — introduction to a group — mutual interests — mutual activity–mutual ideas — control and prevention of any negative contacts outside the group. No rush, no pressure.

III. Special psychotherapy methods: talk + drugs + blondes + alcohol (used for recruitment)

Attention: An alcoholic is more impulsive, untrustful and unreliable; he demonstrates a poverty of ideas and incapacity for attention. He usually has serious personality maladjustments. He's immature, insecure, oversensitive and anxious. Without alcohol he's unable to meet and enjoy people socially, and suffers from marked feeling of inferiority. Besides, alcoholics suffer from vitamin B1 deficiency, which leads to anatomic changes in the central nervous system and heart with symptoms like anorexia, fatigability, and sleep disturbances. Other common symptoms are irritability, poor memory, inability to concentrate, heart pain.

IV. "Transfer" (the object is placed in a regular hospital and then he's transferred to a mental health clinic or jail). In jail you can use such methods an accelerated work schedule (to exhaust the object), turning him into a number to traumatize his psyche, physical punishment or a threat of punishment to keep the object tense and depressed; senseless labor to destroy his personality. Remember: the lower the intellectual level of the object, the more aggressive he is and more sensitive to incentive or punishment.
You can actually re-organize any object's behavior by combining rewards and punishments, exposing him to feared situations and teaching him an instinct of a total (political) obedience.
Imprisonment is a very strong (sometimes — ultimate) tool. My friend who spent 10 years in jail described the changes in his behavior like this:

1st year — aggression as self-defense method (to survive)
2nd year — less personal tension, attempts to adapt the mind and body to the new, isolated way of life
3rd, 4th, 5th — gaining some inside status
6th, 7th — life in jail looks like natural routine
10th — euphoria before gaining freedom

3. Blackmail
Used to force a person to do something (or stop the action) against his will; it's used also for recruitment. Blackmail methods include:
1. Leaking "dirt" on the object through media
2. Creating problems in his personal life and career
3. Straight blackmail (threatening to make public certain compromising facts about him)
4. Placing weapons, drugs, secret documents in object's house or office, followed by search and arrest
5. Accusations of rape (robbery) (use hookers for that)
6. Blackmail by pressing family members. Careful, object may commit suicide after intense blackmail, especially if he is an intellectual

Murders
Regular
Shooting, explosives or poison (cyanides, curare). Use a sniper or a "mouse" car (loaded with explosives and parked on the object's route) if access to the object is impossible because of high security. Anyway, the murder is obvious and investigation is inevitable.

General scheme
The best thing to do is to recruit or "install" somebody with access to the object's security system and get information on his schedule (plus health and habits), places where he likes to relax. Try to gain access to his phone.
Then prepare the plan and train three groups: surveillance (with optics and radios), action (includes snipers, explosives technicians or staged accidents specialists), and security (these

people neutralize bodyguards, witnesses and other people who could interrupt the action; they complete the action if the action group fails; and they can neutralize the action group later, if planned so; they "cover" the safe retreat of action group and "cut" the chase).

For some operations you can modify the ammunition to make it more deadly – hollow cuts in the tip of the bullets will cause the lead to fragment upon impact, making a huge exit hole. You reach same effect using bullets with a drop of mercury in a hollow tip and you can also coat bullets with arsenic or cyanide. Use depleted, non-radioactive uranium bullets (uranium is much heavier than lead – it can be used to make a bullet with a smaller slug and a larger portion of explosive). Teflon bullets are good because with Teflon's antifriction characteristics they pierce bullet proof vests.

Complex
Staged accidents (suicides, catastrophes, drowning or fall, robbery or rape followed by murder, technical accident (fire, electricity, gas), drugs, weapons, poison, explosives misuse. Also, staged natural death (stroke, heart attack, chronic illness as a result of using special technical devices like **irradiation**).

This instruction was written in 1996. CIA used it to kill Palestinian leader Arafat - murdered with radioactive polonium.

Reuters, November 6, 2013
Palestinian leader Yasser Arafat was poisoned to death in 2004 with radioactive polonium, his widow Suha said on Wednesday after receiving the results of Swiss forensic tests on her husband's

corpse." We are revealing a real crime, a political assassination," she told Reuters in Paris.

A team of experts, including from Lausanne University Hospital's Institute of Radiation Physics, opened Arafat's grave in the West Bank city of Ramallah last November, and took samples from his body to seek evidence of alleged poisoning.

"This has confirmed all our doubts," said Suha Arafat after the Swiss forensic team handed over its report to her lawyers and Palestinian officials in Geneva on Tuesday. "It is scientifically proved that he didn't die a natural death and we have scientific proof that this man was killed."

An investigation by the Qatar-based Al Jazeera television news channel first reported last year that traces of polonium-210 were found on personal effects of Arafat given to his widow by the French military hospital where he died. That led French prosecutors to open an investigation for suspected murder in August 2012 at the request of Suha Arafat. Forensic experts from Switzerland, Russia and France all took samples from his corpse for testing after the Palestinian Authority agreed to open his mausoleum. Professor David Barclay, a British forensic scientist retained by Al Jazeera to interpret the results of the Swiss tests, said the findings from Arafat's body confirmed last year's results from traces of bodily fluids on his underwear, toothbrush and clothing. "In my opinion, it is absolutely certain that the cause of his illness was polonium poisoning," Barclay told Reuters. "The levels present in him are sufficient to have caused death.

Al Jazeera said the levels of polonium found in Arafat's ribs, pelvis and in soil that absorbed his remains were at least 18 times higher than normal.

The same radioactive substance was slipped into a cup of tea in a London hotel to kill defecting Russian spy Alexander Litvinenko in 2006. From his deathbed, Litvinenko accused Russian President Vladimir Putin of ordering his murder. The British government refused to hold a public inquiry into his death after ministers withheld some material which could have shed light on Russia's suspected involvement.

Barclay said the type of polonium discovered in Arafat's body must have been manufactured in a nuclear reactor. While many countries could have been the source, someone in Arafat's immediate entourage must have slipped a miniscule dose of the deadly isotope probably as a powder into his drink, food, eye drops or toothpaste, he said.

Arafat fell ill in October 2004, displaying symptoms of acute gastroenteritis with diarrhea and vomiting. At first Palestinian officials said he was suffering from influenza. He was flown to Paris in a French government plane but fell into a coma shortly after his arrival at the Percy military hospital in the suburb of Clamart, where he died on November 11. The official cause of death was a massive stroke but French doctors said at the time they were unable to determine the origin of his illness. No autopsy was carried out. Barclay said no one would have thought to look for polonium as a possible poison until the Litvinenko case, which occurred two years after Arafat's death.

The Al Jazeera investigation was spearheaded by investigative journalist Clayton Swisher, a former U.S. Secret Service bodyguard who became friendly with Arafat and was suspicious of the manner of his death.

"Illegal" spies

When I talk about "the best," I mean the highest intelligence level — illegal spies, intelligence operatives who are secretly deployed abroad and covertly operate there under assumed names and well-documented cover stories, masquerading as native citizens. It's very important if you get, for example, original birth certificate of American citizen, who died (at young age preferably) or any records and documents on him (birth, wedding, death, any IDs, etc.).

The process of training and "installing" such officer is rather complex and includes:

    a) Special training. Foreign language, general, political and special (espionage and counter-espionage) knowledge of the target country; personal cover story — new biography, special technical devices, recruitment methods). Up to three years.

    b) Illegal probation period abroad. A trip abroad through intermediate countries with numerous changes of passports and cover stories, jobs, personal connections. Then he gets to the target country, stays there for another 1-2 years and goes back to his country for additional training and correction of cover story — actually, it's his first combat assignment. The most important part of this assignment is to check the reliability of the cover story and documents; the cover story has to be reinforced with new and old true facts, like short-term studies at universities or professional training courses).

c) Intermediate legislation. On his way back the officer could stay in an intermediate country for another 1-2 years, make contacts with business, scientists, government employees, celebrities.

d) Basic legislation. Officer comes to the target country, obtains genuine documents, gets a job which allows him to travel and talk to many people, recruit informants thus creating an illegal station.

The illegal is usually supplied with a variety of cover documents to make him "invisible" for counter-intelligence — some are used only to cross the borders on the way to a target country, others — to live there, other documents — only for travel to "third countries" to meet with officers of legal or illegal stations or to be used in case of urgent recall to home country (in that case the illegal is supposed to transit at least two or three countries). His further activity depends on how professional counter-espionage service is working in the country.

He could fail in his mission also because of:
- poor training and low quality documents
- neglecting security rules.
- one mistake in pronunciation can give you away
- treason (traitor-informant or a "mole" inside his own service)
- low personal security level (while working with sources)

If we talk about "legal plants", KGB (and modern Russian SVR) loves to recruit Harvard, Yale and Columbia students and "push" them to the top of American politics – US Congress, the White House, the Cabinet.

Coup d'état

Coups, like war, are one of the most violent tools of special services and one could be artificially staged in a target country by "feeding" and "pushing" the political opposition or by using VIP agents in the government. Most coups are "Bureaucratic," and entail mainly a change of leader, usually by person #2. That person might be the trigger or might be induced to practice "passive sabotage" and allow certain others to take over. It is also an example of political engineering. Coups usually use the power of the existing government for its own takeover.

Conditions for a successful coup:
-   the army is supportive or at least neutral (a coup usually involves control of some active
-   portion of the military while neutralizing the remainder of the armed services)
-   the leader is out of town (vacation, visit abroad) or is ill
-   a political or economic crisis.
-   opponents fail to dislodge the plotters, allowing them to consolidate their position, obtain the surrender or acquiescence of the populace, and claim legitimacy

Military Coup

Changing a civilian government to a military one usually in developing countries.

Conditions: a long-term political and economic crisis that threatens national security and the unity of the country. Military chief(s) eventually let the people elect a civilian president and form a civilian government after "re-construction" of political and economic systems. They usually leave for themselves the right to control further political process. A good example is the attempt of anti-Nazi officers to assassinate Hitler in a coup. On July 20, 1944, Colonel Claus Schenk von Stauffenberg brought a bomb-laden suitcase into a briefing room where Hitler was holding a meeting. The bomb exploded and several persons were killed. Hitler was wounded, but his life was saved when the suitcase was unwittingly moved away by someone. Hitler was shielded from the blast by the conference table, leaving him with minor injuries. Subsequently about 5,000 people were arrested by the Gestapo and about 200, including Stauffenberg, were executed in connection with attempt, some on the very same day (which means that Himmler was involved and knew perfectly well about the coup).

"Democratic" Coup
A democratic coup would be a change of the government by the most aggressive (nationalistic) political party.

Conditions:
- artificial or actual government crisis
- mass anti-government propaganda
- organized "democratic" movement all over the country
- provoked mass protests (10,000 participants and up) and civil disobedience actions

To provoke a mass anti-government meeting you have to bring to the place well-trained group of agitators (bring as many as you can), and they will inevitably attract an equal number of curious persons who seek adventures and emotions, as well as those unhappy with the government (unemployed people, young and old, are usually very supportive). Arrange transportation of the participants to take them to meeting places in private or public vehicles. Design placards, flags and banners with different radical slogans or key words; prepare flyers, pamphlets (with instructions for the participants), posters and signs (to make the concentration more noticeable). It's good if you place a surveillance team on the top floors of the nearby buildings – they will report any changes in the event; have also messengers to transmit your orders. Remember, if you clash with police and military and a participant(s) is being killed, the conflict inflames right away.

Your people can also infiltrate the spontaneous anti-government meeting and turn it into a mass radical demonstration with fights and incidents. Key agitators (with security attached to them) have to be dispersed and stand by placards, signs, lampposts; they have to avoid places of disturbances, once they have provoked them.

- the leader of the meeting must be protected by a ring of bodyguards (they protect him from police or help him to escape).
- government buildings must be "covered" by a blockade
- "Democratic" nationalistic coup in Ukraine (2004), so-called "orange revolution". Scenario: acts of civil disobedience, strikes, sit-ins (in the central square), aggressive propaganda, mass demands to re-vote the 2004 Ukrainian presidential election.

Revolution

A change of government and political and economic systems by political gangsters, usually fed, pushed, incited, and possibly funded and equipped by the secret services of another country. (Even the American Revolution would not have succeeded without French military advisors and financial support.) Government buildings are blockaded, the government isolated, all communications and transportation systems captured, government media closed, new government formed.

Conditions:
- political and economic crisis
- mass anti-government propaganda (in the army too)-provoked mass protests and civil disobedience actions - terror and urban guerillas

Self-coup

The current government assumes extraordinary powers not allowed by the legislation. It often happens when the president is democratically elected, but later takes control of the legislative and judicial powers.

Surveillance

Actual espionage is not what you see in the movies and you have absolutely no chance of evasion if a real professional surveillance crew is following you. Why? Because they use multiple methods and mixed methods.

Physical surveillance
Methods
"One line" – officers follow the object forming a line behind him and passing him one by one.
"Two lines" – officers form two lines on both sides of the street.
"Circle" – officers block the area and start searching (used in case they lose the object).
"Fork" – one officer (a car) moves in front of the object, another one — behind, other officers (cars) move along parallel streets
 "Box" – used when the object enters supermarket, hotel, restaurant. One or two officers follow the object; the others wait for him at the exits.
"Demonstration" – officers demonstrate their presence to press the object and lower his activity.
"Provocation" – officers attack the object, beat him, steal (secret) documents. Often used to lower his activity if he's trying to play James Bond.
"Outstrip" – officers do not follow the object because they know exactly where he's going.
 "Football" – officers pass the object to each other (car — a group — bicyclist — car…)
 "Movie" – the crew watches the object in stages: first day — to the subway only, second day — from subway to his office, etc. (used abroad). The crew has to have a female member if they are watching a woman (she could use the ladies room for a secret meeting) and members of various ethnicities (white, black, Latino) because the object could go to a specific ethnic area.

If you're the object and you've noticed surveillance:
-   Don't rush, move at the same speed.
-   Relax at the nearest bar (and relax the crew).
-   Don't show how professional you are by trying to disappear, otherwise they could intensify surveillance or even neutralize you (smash your car, beat you up).
-   Postpone the operation you were engaged in.

- Use a "draught" if you need to see your agent no matter what. Change lanes (if you are driving), stop the car and then drive left or right.
- If you don't see surveillance, that means either there's no surveillance or you've failed in counter-surveillance. Discreetly watch the agent who's coming to meet you and try to detect any possible surveillance; or you may have been "outstripped."

Surveillance crew mistakes:
- The same crew follows the object all day long.
- The object "rules" the crew and calculates it (he moves faster — the crew moves faster).
- A crew member is too noticeable (unusual dress, haircut, disabled parts of the body, too fat or too skinny, too ugly or too pretty).
- The crew starts to search possible hiding places for espionage evidence right after the object leaves (and he may be watching).
- The crew leaves traces after a secret search of the object's house (office).
- The crew does not report its mistakes or the fact that they've lost the object.
- The crew is not professional (using childish tricks like jumping out of a subway train just before the doors close).

Technical Surveillance
1. Visual surveillance. Done through special holes in the ceilings and walls, through the windows from the opposite building (car) or by installing the camera inside the house (you can substitute something, like a clock, for the same thing but "stuffed" with a camera or recorder.) You can use informant as well to watch the object outside his house (especially if you want to do a secret search).

2. Listening devices. The easiest thing is to listen to the object's phone (record all calls, including those dialed "by mistake"). If you work inside his apartment, make sure you equip the room

where he usually talks. Attention: avoid widespread mistake when your agent keeps the listening device on his body; install a miniature device in his clothes or shoes, because the object could try a test and ask the agent to take off his clothes or invite him to the sauna or pool.

3. If you are working abroad, listen 24/7 to local counterintelligence surveillance radiofrequencies.

4. Reading the mail. When you control the object's mail, remember he could use multiple addresses and PO boxes. Open all the letters with no return address or PO box. Watch when you open the letter — the object could leave a tiny piece of paper, hair, etc. to check if anybody opened the letter. Analyze the text carefully — there could be a cipher or the words with double meaning (jargon), especially when you read mafia mail.

5. Combination of above-mentioned methods

Spies Identification
If a spy is an intelligence officer working abroad under "cover" (diplomat, businessman, and reporter) you can identify him by:
- following the careers of all diplomats who work at your enemy's embassies all over the world
- recruiting a "mole" inside the intelligence service (or inside the station)
- setting up your agent for recruitment by the enemy's station
- watching foreigners who try to make discreet contacts with native citizens with access to secrets
- making a model of a spy (professional behavior, attempts to detect surveillance, attempts to recruit sources or just get any classified information during normal meetings, "throwing away" money trying to get access to government employees, military and scientific circles)
- using secret surveillance and listening devices inside the station and practicing secret searches

If a spy is an intelligence officer working in your country under "cover" of a native citizen (or he is recruited by a native citizen) you identify him by making a model (contacts with identified spies — that's often the only sign which points out a spy, and that's why surveillance is very important in getting information from a "mole"). CIA "mole" and KGB intelligence officer V. Martynov arrested at Moscow airport, 1987.

"Moles"

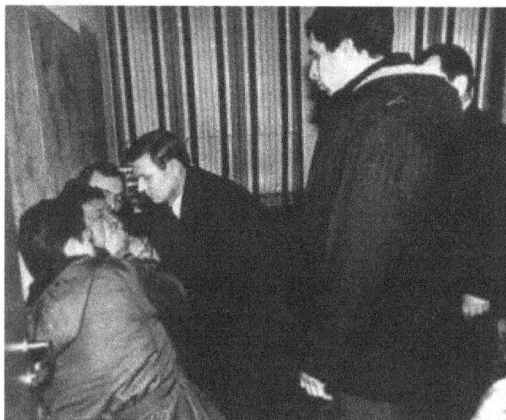

CIA "mole" and KGB intelligence officer V. Martynov arrested at Moscow airport, 1987.

A "mole" is a spy inside the government, recruited or "installed" most often within the special services, by an outside government/agency. The 3 most dangerous things a "mole" can do:
-   Calculate President's plans and decisions judging by information he's asking for.
-   Manipulate information being sent to President, and thus influence global political decisions
-   Paralyze to some extent the government (if he's CIA or FBI Director)

Methods to detect a "mole":
A. Use index cards (special file) — never use computers to save this information!

Prepare a file on each officer and mark there the signs of a "mole" — has or spends too much money, asks too many extra questions; uses professional skills to check for physical and technical surveillance; has discreet contacts with foreigners; discreet copying of top secret documents; attempts to get a job in most secret departments; talks with close friends and family members about the possibility of making money as a "mole"; behavior deviations — extra suspiciousness, excitement, depression, drugs or alcohol addiction. Three signs are enough to start an investigation — the "triangulation" principle.

B. Use provocation. If a prospective "mole" is looking for a contact with the enemy and is ready to betray, and you have exact information, organize such a "meeting" for him. Do not arrest the person right away — play along, as he may give you connections to other people who are ready to betray. There's one more provocation method: you supply the suspects with "highly classified information" and just watch what they do.

C. Use "filter" or "narrowing the circle." Include all the officers you suspect in a "circle" and narrow it until one name is left as the most likely suspect.

D. Make a "model" of a "mole," judging by information you have on him.

E. Recruit an insider. Recruit a "mole" inside your enemy's intelligence service and he'll help you to find the one inside yours (it's called "grabbing the other end of a thread").

F. Don't trust anybody.

What to Do If You Detect a "Mole"
- assess the damage
- restrict his access to classified information and start "feeding" him with fake data
- stop all operations he was involved in and create the illusion they are still in progress

- bring home officers and agents who work abroad and had contacts with him and those to whose files he had access
- start 24/7 surveillance if you've decided to play the game and look into his contacts
- arrest the "mole" discreetly (if you want to continue the game)
- Effective methods to prevent treason do not exist.

How to Cover Your "Mole"

There are special methods to cover your own "mole" and a "switch" is the most effective — it's when you "switch" counterintelligence to other, innocent persons who work with the "mole." You can try information "leaks" through a "double agent" — it looks like you receive top secret information through another traitor or by breaking the electronic security systems. Or you can try information "leak" through publications in big newspapers — it looks like information is not secret and is known to many people or there's another "mole."

Special Strategies

Every operation demands a set of original methods, especially if we are talking about strategic intelligence. I give you a few examples.

1. "Domino" or "chain reaction." A coup, revolution or civil war in one country provokes the same actions in other countries (neighbors). It doesn't matter what country is going to be next, most important – what country is a target.

2. "False flag". The planned, but never executed, 1962 Operation Northwoods plot by the U.S. administration for a war with Cuba involved scenarios such as hijacking a passenger plane and blaming it on Cuba.

3. "Sliding" strategy. Transformation of a secret operation into an open one: support of illegal opposition/coup.

4. "Restriction." You damage (limit) international and economic connections (projects) of the enemy.

5. "Monopoly." Special operation to keep country's monopoly or status as economic leader or special (nuclear) holder, or high tech producer. Includes actions to restrict the attempts of other countries to get strategic raw materials and modern weapons and technologies.

6. "Reverse effect." The government declares a certain goal and launches a military or special operation, but the result is something quite different, possibly opposite. Examples: instead of separating (ethnic) group "A" from group "B" both of them are being exterminated; instead of peace and democracy in a certain region, power is being concentrated in one group and the opposition is being exterminated.

7. "Clash." You "clash" the government and opposition of a target country and support civil war until the country is ruined and you get it for free.

8. "Salami-slice strategy". It's a process of threats and alliances used to overcome opposition. It includes the creation of several factions within the opposing political party, and then dismantling that party from inside, without causing the "sliced" sides to protest.

9. "Positive shock." A domestic operation; to save the government during a crisis, special service provokes artificial civil conflict or sabotage, imitation (terror), and the government takes care of the "problem."

10. "Controlled crisis export" (see "Foreign Policy")

11. "Sanitation border." "Fencing" the target country by enemies (neighbors).

12. "Alibi." You build a "chain" of evidence (witnesses) and move the investigation to a dead end.

13. "Passive sabotage." A very effective strategy used to cover up a major action like the assassination of a President or the destruction of several office towers. You just "do not see the bad guys" who are going to kill the President or blow up the city. In any case you win — the perpetrators are not sure you are watching them; you can arrest them if the object survives or liquidate them once the object is dead. You don't need a big conspiracy, you just give the order to ignore certain people until their plan materializes.

14. "Special tour." You help the target country to "build democratic institutions" (the government and local administrations) by sending official crews to help. Actually, they rule the country and that's a "hidden occupation."

15. "Mask." You mask your actual global plans (reforms) by another big action (war).

16. Illegal espionage operations. Very dangerous, because illegal spy is playing born American and can make career in business, becoming #1 Pentagon supplier or in the government, getting to the Congress or even White House.

Instructions for FBI
"Golden rules"
1. Don't die a hero – that's bad planning, poor training and lack of experience; the dead man goes to a hall of shame and stupidity. Bad planning is an operational failure; once things have gone off track it is far more complicated to achieve the objective. Multi-step complex operations come from the fantasies of bureaucrats who watch too many movies. Keep it simple if you want to get it right.

2. Never provoke people to break the law – that's not professional.

3. Always look for insider if it's about sophisticated operation (bank robbery, etc.).

Investigation
Stages:
- secure and examine carefully the crime scene (every person who enters the scene is a potential destroyer of physical evidence)
- record the scene (make photos, sketches, notes with detailed written description of the scene with the location of evidences recovered)
- collect physical evidences (blood, semen, saliva, hair, documents, drugs, weapons and explosives, poisonous substances, fingerprints, traces, soils and minerals, fiber) and package everything
- collect confessions and eyewitnesses accounts and then
- make a plan of investigation and correct it later
- research similar crimes and criminals involved
- make a model (profile) of the suspect
- analyze expertise data
- work with secret sources
- cooperate with other divisions (abroad, if needed)
- make arrest
- interrogate

Arrest
In daytime arrest people discreetly — don't bring extra public irritation. There's a general rule: more arrests — less crime prevention (after being in jail people, engage in more sophisticated and secret criminal activity). After mass arrests at certain places (buildings) repeat the action in a day or two.

Procedure:
- chasing the object, block the area into circles (follow the plan for a certain area) and try to "push" him to a certain place where your team is waiting

- taking the object in the street: look around for his partner(s), who could shoot you from behind
- be on the alert if anybody tries to talk to you in the street — it could be an attempt to divert your attention
- arresting a crew, shoot and disarm any people with guns first
- never hesitate to shoot terrorists — some of them have mental problems and won't think a second before shooting you
- arrest a dangerous object while he's relaxed (drugs, alcohol, sex, sleep) and don't let him kill himself, eliminate evidences or warn his partners. (Most people feel more relaxed when traveling abroad.) To take the object alive, scream, shoot over his head, use smoke and light grenades.
- camouflage your team (as ambulance workers, construction workers, vendors, etc.)
- if there's a crowd around the object, shoot in the air and order everybody to lie down— the object has no choice
- if the object is well armed and very dangerous (and you have intelligence information on that), you have to shoot him even in a very crowded area as you never know what he's going to do next — take hostages, shoot people or blow up a bomb (three wounded people is a better score than three hundred dead).

Interrogation
Interrogation is a conversational process of information gathering. The intent of interrogation is to control an individual so that he will either willingly supply the requested information or, if someone is an unwilling participant in the process, to make the person submit to the demands for information.

Remember, people tend to:
- talk when they are under stress and respond to kindness and understanding.
- show deference when confronted by superior authority. This is culturally dependent, but in most areas of the

world people are used to responding to questions from a variety of government and quasi-government officials.

- operate within a framework of personal and culturally derived values. People tend to respond positively to individuals who display the same value system and negatively when their core values are challenged.
- respond to physical and, more importantly, emotional self-interest.
- fail to apply or remember lessons they may have been taught regarding security if confronted with a disorganized or strange situation
- be more willing to discuss a topic about which the interrogator demonstrates identical or related experience or knowledge
- appreciate flattery and exoneration from guilt

Tricks:

a. "good cop / bad cop"
b. "story under a story" (after intense interrogation the object tells a different story — which is not true, either)
c. "bombing" with questions
d. pressure by not interrogating
e. "silence makes your situation worse" trick
f. "admit one small episode and that's it" trick
g. "I help you — you help me" trick
h. "shift" – try to shift the blame away from the suspect to some other person or set of circumstances that prompted the subject to commit the crime. That is, develop themes containing reasons that will justify or excuse the crime. Themes may be developed or changed to find one to which the accused is most responsive.

President's Protection (Instructions for Secret Service)

The top priority in protecting the President's life must be organized and complete intelligence. Any information from any person from any country concerning the President's personal security has to be immediately analyzed, and immediate action has to be performed. This is the first priority for intelligence and counter-intelligence agencies and police as well as the Secret Service. If the system is organized properly, nobody could even get in a position to try to shoot. Of course, the safest thing is to restrict the President's routes to government buildings only; but he has to travel and he has to travel abroad, too. Still, the President should leave his Office only when he really has to.

Since the President has to be let out from time to time, the newer technique is to restrict where the onlookers may congregate, especially those who wish to take the opportunity to express dismay with Presidential policies. Thus we now see the evolution of "free speech corners" so that demonstrators are confined to specific areas far from the actual event where the President is appearing or the route he is transiting.

Practical Protection during Presidential Appearances

1. The Secret Service must have a top-secret plan of all visits, because the advance group has to come to the place at least a week ahead and cooperate with the field FBI offices and police (foreign special services if it's a visit abroad) paying attention to extremist groups and organizations. Officers and technicians search the place, looking for possible explosives, radioactive, biological and chemical dangerous or poisonous stuff and weapons; they check the walls, floors and ceilings; check air and water in the area; install weapons and explosives detectors and stay at the place 24/7, using night vision devices, too. (Dogs are good helpers if there is any question of explosives.) You have to check nearby houses as well (there could be people with mental health problems or dangerous criminals. Remember, the President must not appear in open areas close to apartment buildings. And the President has to be able to reach the National Security Command Center at any time.

2. If the President has to make a speech in open area there should be at least 3 security circles around him:
   - up to 50 ft (personal bodyguards, weapons and explosives technicians)
   - up to 200 ft (fast reaction anti-terror group)
   - up to 1000 ft (support groups, snipers, police)

The security system includes both "open" and undercover groups (obvious security and people who play the crowd or service — drivers, waiters, cleaners — terrorists don't pay attention to them, as a rule). Each group follows its instructions strictly and avoids mess (personal bodyguards are in charge of immediate protection, anti-terror group has to fight and chase terrorists, etc.). Extra people always mean extra danger, so the most secure situation is when extra people have no access to the President at all and can't get into any of three circles. The guest list has to be triple checked to exclude anybody with criminal records who could compromise the leader. Reporters are there too and you have to tell them exactly where to wait (they have to be checked and kept separate after that), where to stand and what pictures (poses) to take; the President can't look stupid or funny. Inside the building watch when people applaud, stand up and sit down — terrorists prefer these situations to shoot or blow explosives.

When the President moves through or along the crowd, "cut" it into pieces, guard him in circles, watch people who are carrying any objects (no flowers!) — they must not approach him; watch people with hands in their pockets, those who try to touch him, shake his hand, pass any object (gift, picture, photo). They must not be allowed to do that. If anybody behaves in a suspicious way, hold him tight (so he can't take out a gun) and "screw" him out of the crowd. In case of any attempt push the President to the ground, cover him and shoot immediately. Then leave the place as soon as possible and bring him to the hospital for a checkup (even if he's OK).

The worst one – Secret Service and other agencies get inadequate intelligence information on a possible attempt or overlook important information, including anonymous letters and mail from psychos. (They must have information, even if it's "inside" the White House conspiracy. Agents have to memorize pictures of all the most dangerous persons who are wanted in the United States and people who were involved in attempted attacks on top politicians worldwide.)

The next two — extraneous people are allowed access to the President or extraneous people stay in the area close enough to shoot the President. In 1997, a France Press reporter took a picture of the Clintons dancing during their vacation on the Virgin Islands — they were dressed for the Caribbean and were happy in their privacy. Luckily, it was just a reporter, but what if it had been a sniper? What was the Secret Service doing? Then the picture was published worldwide and Hillary Clinton was furious – she didn't look attractive at all.

The last two major errors occur when (1) you can't identify the potential terrorists in the crowd and (2) you react too slow or waste time evacuating the President.

CHAPTER 3
Military Management

Commander-in–Chief

American presidents love war, not peace, because:

a) Successful military engagement enhances presidential popularity. All five Presidents who have run for re-election during a war have won.

b) A quick war improves the electoral fortunes of the president's political party.

c) War is good business, at least if you win, and at least if it does not drag on too long. It stimulates demand for a variety of manufactured goods and services (even if they are all destined to go down the drain) and is a powerful stimulus to all fields of scientific endeavor.

d) War provides opportunities to direct lucrative contracts to companies and individuals who helped get the President elected, or who can help in the future; and to the constituents of select Senators and Congressmen for the same reasons.

e) War usually pleases the Joint Chiefs (and their full support is important politically).

f) War keeps down the unemployment figures.

g) War is just one detail in a vast ongoing game of international strategy for domination; it is as much a financial operation as anything else.

h) War unifies the country, and keeps the public's attention away from issues that might be controversial.

i) War provides a rationale for the implementation of tighter legislation and the removal of certain freedoms that would never be tolerated in peacetime America.

At the same time, war is limited by political decisions and by public opinion. Initially the use of US forces spurs a "rally around the flag" effect that lifts the President's popularity and builds up support for the troops. But the American people are casualty averse and the positive effect lasts only until the number of casualties and the length of the engagement begin to wear on the public. Continued military action will then have a deleterious effect on presidential approval ratings as the war becomes increasingly unpopular.

In the long run, the destruction of such vast quantities of resources, and the diversion of so much of the nation's productive capacity away from actual goods and services for the real economy, are obviously immensely deleterious. Eventually, these downside effects will begin to dawn on even the best-manipulated electorate.

Sniper
"Golden" rules

1. Train your muscles to snap to the standard position for shooting, to squeeze the trigger straight back with the ball of your finger to avoid jerking the gun sideways.

Train yourself to shoot while you stand, sit, lie, walk, run, jump, fall down; shoot at voices, shoot in a dark room, different weather and distance, day and night; shoot one object and a group; use one gun, two guns, gun and submachine gun (some doctrines train a sniper to breathe deeply before shooting, then hold their lungs empty while he lines up and takes his shot; other go further, teaching a sniper to shoot between heartbeats to minimize barrel motion)

2. Camouflage yourself ten times before you make a single shot. Position yourself in a building (no rooftops or churches!), which

offers a long-range fields of fire and all-round observation. Don't stay in places with heavy traffic! Use unusual angles of approach and frequent slow movement to prevent accurate counter-attacks.

3. Move slowly to prevent accurate counter-attack, don't be a mark yourself

4. Kill officers and military leaders first (Attention, officers: don't walk in front of your soldiers!)

5. Use suppressive fire to cover a retreat

6. Use rapid fire when the squad attempts a rescue

7. Shoot helicopters, turbine disks of parked jet fighters, missile guidance packages, tubes or wave guides of radar sets

8. At distances over 300 m attempt body shots, aiming at the chest; at lesser distances attempt head shots (the most effective range is 300 to 600 meters). Police snipers who generally engage at much shorter distances may attempt head shots to ensure the kill (in instant-death hostage situations they shoot for the cerebellum, a part of the brain that controls voluntary movement that lies at the base of the skull).

9. Shoot from flanks and rear

10. Never approach the body until you shoot it several times

11. Careful: the object could be wearing a bulletproof vest

12. It's important to get to the place, but it's more important to get out alive

13. Remember, in hot weather bullets travel higher, in cold — lower; a silencer reduces the maximum effective range of the weapon. Wind poses the biggest problem — the stronger the wind, the more difficult it is to hold the rifle steady and gauge

how it will affect the bullet's trajectory. (You must be able to classify the wind and the best method is to use the clock system. With you at the center of the clock and the target at 12 o'clock, the wind is assigned into three values: full, half and no value. Full value means that the force of the wind will have a full effect on the flight of the bullet, and these winds come from 3 and 9 o'clock. Half value means that a wind at the same speed, but from 1, 2, 4, 5, 7, 8, 10 and 11 o'clock, will move the bullet only half as much as a full-value wind. No value means that a wind from 6 or 12 o'clock will have little or no effect on the flight of the bullet). Shooting uphill or downhill can require more adjustment due to the effects of gravity. For moving targets, the point of aim is in front of the target (it's called "Leading" the target, where the amount of lead depends on the speed and angle of the target's movement. For this technique, holding over is the preferred method. Anticipating the behavior of the target is necessary to accurately place the shot).

14. NEVER fire from the edge of a wood line – you should fire from a position inside the wood line (in the shade of shadows).

15. DO NOT cause overhead movement of trees, bushes or tall grasses by rubbing against them; move very slowly.

16. Do not use trails, roads or footpaths, avoid built-up and populated areas and areas of heavy enemy guerrilla activity.

17. If you work in terrain without any natural support, use your rucksack, sandbag, a forked stick, or you may build a field-expedient bipod or tripod. The most accurate position though is prone, with a sandbag supporting the stock, and the stock's cheek-piece against the cheek.

18. The sniper has a tendency to watch the target instead of his aiming point.

Counter-sniper tactics

1. Active: direct observation by posts equipped with laser protective glasses and night vision devices; patrolling with military working dogs; calculating the trajectory; bullet triangulation; using decoys to lure a sniper; using another sniper; UAV (unmanned aerial vehicles); directing artillery or mortar fire onto suspected sniper positions, the use of smoke-screens; emplacing tripwire-operated munitions, mines, or other booby-traps near suspected sniper positions(you can improvise booby-traps by connecting trip-wires to fragmentation hand grenades, smoke grenades or flares. Even though these may not kill the sniper, they will reveal his location. Booby –traps devices should be placed close to likely sniper hides or along the probable routes used into and out of the sniper's work area). If the squad is pinned down by sniper fire and still taking casualties, the order may be given to rush the sniper's position. If the sniper is too far for a direct rush, a "rush to cover" can also be used. The squad may take casualties, but with many moving targets and a slow-firing rifle, the losses are usually small compared to holding position and being slowly picked off. If the sniper's position is known, but direct retaliation is not possible, a pair of squads can move through concealment (cover) and drive the nipper toward the group containing the targets. This decreases the chances that the sniper will find a stealthy, quick escape route.

2. Passive: limited exposure of the personnel (use concealed routes, avoid plazas and intersections, stay away from doorways and windows, move along the side of the street and not down the center, move in the shadows, move dispersed, avoid lighted areas at night, move quickly across open areas, avoid wearing obvious badges of rank, adapt screens on windows, use armored vehicles); use Kevlar helmet and bulletproof vest.

Military tricks

1. Use rapid dominance: technology + speed + information domination.

2. Use artillery preparation. It is the artillery fire delivered before an attack to destroy, neutralize, or suppress the enemy's defense and to disrupt communications and disorganize the enemy's defense.

3. Use deception especially before the first strike (air strike + artillery). Deception plays a key part in offensive operations and has two objectives: the first objective is to weaken the local defense by drawing reserves to another part of the battlefield. This may be done by making a small force seem larger than it is. The second objective is to conceal the avenue of approach and timing of the main attack.

4. Imitate assault to make the enemy expose his positions and fire system.

5. Mines, mines, mines. There are four types of minefield : the tactical large-area minefield, usually laid by engineers, for tactical use on the battlefield(i.e. to canalize the enemy into killing areas); the protective minefield, the sort that you will plant in front of your position for defensive purposes; the nuisance minefield, designed to hamper and disrupt enemy movement ; and the dummy minefield – a wired off area suitably marked can be as effective as the real thing.

6. Don't touch anything in the places the enemy just left — check for mines first. A minefield is a mortal surprise and you have to know how to breach and cross it: remove your helmet, rucksack, watch, belt, and anything else that may hinder movement or fall off, leave your rifle and equipment with another soldier in the team, get a wooden stick about 30 cm (12 in) long for a probe and sharpen one of the ends (do not use a metal probe), place the unsharpened end of the probe in the palm of one hand with your fingers extended and your thumb holding the probe, and probe every 5 cm (2 in) across a 1-meter area in front of you and push the probe gently into the ground at an angle less than 45 degrees, kneel (or lie down) and feel upward and forward with your free hand to find tripwires and pressure prongs before starting to

probe, put enough pressure on the probe to sink it slowly into the ground and if the probe does not go into the ground, pick or chip the dirt away with the probe and remove it by hand, stop probing when a solid object is touched, remove enough dirt from around the object to find out what it is. If you found a mine, remove enough dirt around it to see what type of mine it is, mark it and report its exact location to your leader. Once a footpath has been probed and the mines marked, a security team should cross the minefield to secure the far side. After the far side is secure, the rest of the unit should cross.

7. Visual indicators. Pay attention to the following indicators: trip wires, signs of road repair (new fill or paving, road patches, ditching), dead animals, damaged vehicles, tracks that stop unexplainably, wires leading away from the side of the road (they may be firing wires that are partially buried), mounds of dirt, change of plants color,, pieces of wood or other debris on a road. Remember, mined areas, like other obstacles are often covered by fire. Keep also in mind that local civilians try to avoid certain (mined) areas.

8. Use phony minefields to simulate live minefields. For example, disturb the ground so that it appears that mines have been emplaced and mark boundaries with appropriate warnings.

9. Make a real minefield appear phony, or camouflage it. For example, once a real minefield is settled, a wheel or a specially made circular wooden tank track marker can be run through the field, leaving track or tire marks to lure the enemy onto live mines. Antipersonnel mines should not be sown in such a field until the track marks have been laid. Another method is to leave gaps in the mechanically laid field, run vehicles through the gaps, and then close them with hand-laid mines without disturbing the track marks.

10. Use feint attack to draw defensive action towards the point under assault (it's usually used as a diversion and to force the

enemy to concentrate more manpower in a given area so that the opposing force in another area is weaker).

11. Issue false orders over the radio; imitate a tanks', fighters' and bombers' assault while preparing to retreat.

12. Use dummy units and installations, phony radio traffic, movement and suppressive fires in other areas timed to coincide with the real attack

13. Use force multiplication by using decoy vehicles and use small convoys to generate dust clouds. Move trucks into and out of the area giving it the appearance of being a storage facility or logistic base.

14. Simulate damage to induce the enemy to leave important targets alone. For example, ragged patterns can be painted on the walls and roof of a building with tar and coal dust, and covers placed over them.

15. Stack debris nearby and wire any unused portions for demolition. During an attack, covers are removed under cover of smoke generators, debris scattered and demolitions blown. Subsequent enemy air photography will disclose a building that is too badly damaged to be used.

16. Change positions at night time only.

17. Use dispersal to relocate and spread out forces to increase their chances of survival.

18. Imitate fake ballistic missiles divisions and military headquarters to entrap enemy's intelligence and sabotage groups.

19. Use "sack" strategy ("cutting" enemy's army into separate groups).

20. Use strategic bombing (the massive attack on cities, industries, lines of communication and supply).

21. Simulate bombing of minor objects and attack important ones.

22. Use counter-battery fire (detecting with counter-battery radars the source of incoming artillery shells and firing back), using mobile artillery pieces or vehicles with mounted rocket launchers to fire and then move before any counter-battery fire can land on the original position.

23. Use airborne operations, when helicopters transport troops into the battle and provide fire support at battle sites simultaneously with artillery fire, keeping enemy off guard.

24. Helicopters are extremely important as they can be sent everywhere: to kill tanks and other helicopters, for aerial mine laying, for electronic warfare, for naval operations (anti-submarine and anti-ship patrols), to correct artillery and tactical fighters fire, for reconnaissance, command, control and communications, to insert special forces, to evacuate casualties (this helps maintain the morale of the troops), to carry supplies (missile systems, ammunition, fuel food, to escort convoys, for navigational help, to destroy battlefield radars, communications and radio relay systems, to seal gaps and protect flanks, for rear-area security, counter — penetration, rapid reinforcement of troops under pressure, raids and assaults behind enemy lines, air assault in offensive and defensive operations, to strengthen anti-tank defenses by inserting infantry anti-tank teams. Helicopters offer a strong tactical surprise and take a ground conflict into the third dimension, making the enemy's ground maneuvers impossible.

25. When fighting an insurgency: once you get intelligence, you have to bomb the area to "soften" insurgents and then send helicopters with special forces teams right away. Helicopters suppress and cut-off by fire insurgents trying to escape and the

teams clear-up the remains. Transport helicopters must bring in troops rapidly from different bases and build-up numerically superior force which insurgents cannot match.

26. Use joint bombers/fighters flights to bomb transportation, supply, bridges, railroads, highways, antiaircraft and radar sites. To gain surprise, attack with the sun behind you. Remember, enemy will try to saturate the airspace through which the aircraft will fly with fire.

27. Watch out for tank ambushes!

Storming the City
Procedure
1. Effective intelligence is 90% of success. Use sources like agents among the enemy's high ranking officers, prisoners of war, captured documents and maps, enemy's activity, local civilians (agents). Use intelligence and sabotage groups (through them you can deliver your fake plans and maps). You must know how the enemy usually defends a built-up area and the approaches to it, critical objectives within the built-up area that provide decisive tactical advantages, tactical characteristics of the built-up area and its structure. Information about the population will assist in determining where to attack, what firepower restrictions may be imposed, and what areas within the urban complex must be avoided to minimize destruction of life-support facilities and civilian casualties.

2. Make the enemy attack you if possible, because if you attack first the victims calculation is 5:1.

3. Train your troops to storm this certain city.

4. Blockade the city completely.

5. Attack the city from different points (flanks and rear !) at the same time after intense artillery fire and bombing (that's a very strong psychological blow. Its intensity is determined by the

strength of defensive forces, the type of building construction, and the density of fires required to suppress observation and fires. You must destroy command posts, heavy weapons positions, communications, troop emplacements, tall structures that permit observation. Then engineers move forward under the cover of smoke and high explosives to neutralize barriers and breach minefields on routes into the city). Field artillery, attack helicopters and offense air support must disrupt the enemy command and control network and destroy his support units (field artillery mostly creates breaches in buildings, walls and barricades. Mortars cover avenues of enemy troop movements, such as street intersections and alleys; mortars firing positions are placed behind walls or inside buildings close to their targets). A hasty attack is conducted when the enemy has not established strong defensive positions and attacking forces can exploit maneuver to overwhelm the defense – locate a weak spot or gap in enemy defenses, fix forward enemy elements, rapidly move through or around the gap or weak spot to be exploited. A deliberate attack is necessary when enemy defenses are extremely prepared, when the urban obstacle is extremely large or severely congested, or when the advantage of surprise has been lost. It's divided into three basic phases: isolation from reinforcement and resupply by securing dominating terrain and utilizing direct and indirect fires; assault to rupture the defenses and secure a foothold on the perimeter of the built-up area from which attacks to clear the area may be launched (an envelopment, assaulting defensive weaknesses on the flanks or rear of the built-up area, is preferred, however, a penetration may be required; and clearance, a systematic building-by-building, block-by-block advance through the entire area..

6. Target vital bridges, transportation facilities that are required to sustain future combat operations, strategic industrial or vital communications facilities. Attacks against built-up areas will be avoided when the area is not required to support future operations, bypassing is tactically feasible, the built-up area has been declared an "open city" to preclude civilian casualties or to

preserve cultural or historical facilities, sufficient combat forces are not available to seize and clear the built-up area.

7. Don't use tanks on narrow streets! Tanks can be decisive in city fighting, with the ability to demolish walls and fire medium and heavy machine guns in several directions simultaneously. However, tanks are especially vulnerable in urban combat. It's much easier for enemy infantry to sneak behind a tank or fire at its sides, where it is vulnerable. In addition, firing down from multi-story buildings allows shots at the soft upper turret armor and even basic weapons like Molotov cocktails, if aimed at the engine air intakes, can disable a tank.

8. Use 3 groups at each point.

1st. A "dead" group plus tanks moves fast to the center, again, after intense artillery fire and bombing (otherwise you'll have heavy casualties).

2nd. The group follows the first one and inside the city goes like a "fan" in all directions enveloping the defender's flanks and rear.

3rd. The group is on reserve in case the enemy counterattacks.

The first phase of the attack should be conducted when visibility is poor. Troops can exploit poor visibility to cross open areas, gain access to rooftops, infiltrate enemy areas and gain a foothold. If the attack must be made when visibility is good, units should consider using smoke to conceal movement. The formation used in attack depends on the width and depth of the zone to be cleared, the character of the area, anticipated enemy resistance, and the formation adopted by the next higher command. Lead companies may have engineers attached for immediate support. Tasks given to engineers may include preparing and using explosives to breach walls and obstacles, finding and exploding mines in place or helping remove them, clearing barricades and rubble, cratering roads.

9. Use paratroopers to capture important objects (airport, government buildings, military headquarters, port, railway station).

10. Capture high buildings and place machine gunners and snipers on upper floors (buildings provide excellent sniping posts for defenders, too).

11. Get all important cross-roads to maneuver troops and tanks.

12. Block highways!

13. Watch out — there are mines everywhere (alleys and rubble-filled streets are ideal for planting booby traps). Be alert for booby traps in doors, windows, halls, stairs, and concealed in furniture.

14. Watch underground communications — the enemy could stay in subway tunnels, sewage system.

15. Don't waste time storming the buildings — blow up the walls and move forward.

16. Soldiers in an urban environment are faced with ground direct fire danger in three dimensions — not just all-round fire but also from above (multi-story buildings) and from below (sewers and subways) and that's why, here, the most survivable systems, like tanks, are at great risk. Also, there are increased casualties because of shattered glass, falling debris, rubble, ricochets, urban fires and falls from heights. Difficulty in maintaining situational awareness also contributes to this problem because of increased risk of fratricide. Stress-related casualties and non-battle injuries resulting from illnesses or environmental hazards, such as contaminated water, toxic industrial materials also increase the number of casualties.

17. In the streets use artillery and mortars to "soften" the enemy up before assault.

National Infrastructure Protection Plan

Department of Homeland Security, 2006

Why it does not work

1. "Future terrorist attacks against critical infrastructure (CI) across the United States could seriously threaten national security, result in mass casualties, weaken the economy and damage public morale and confidence".

Wrong. If terrorists could seriously threaten national security, we have serious problems with national security which means emergency situation. Besides, you implant panic and you, not terrorists, damage public confidence.

2. "It is not practical or feasible to protect all assets, systems and networks against every possible terrorist attack vector".

Wrong. If we have a national security system we must protect everything and everybody from terror. If we do not have it, we have to create and use it "against every possible terrorist vector".

3. "Department of Homeland Security does not have broad regulatory authority over critical infrastructure and cannot compel private sector entities to submit infrastructure or operational information. Rather, DHS works in partnership with industry to identify the necessary information and promote the trusted exchange of such data".

Wrong. Department of Homeland Security must have access to any information if it's vital to national security.

4. "Terrorists may contemplate attacks against the Nation's critical infrastructure to achieve three general types of effects:

- direct infrastructure effects: disruption or arrest of critical functions through direct attacks on an asset, system or network

Wrong. You can't attack directly the system or network, because it's protected by multilevel security system. If it's not protected, it's a small target of no interest.

- indirect infrastructure effects: cascading disruption and financial consequences for the society and economy through public and private sector reactions to an attack

Wrong. What public reaction has financial consequences for the society?

- exploitation of infrastructure: exploitation of elements of a particular infrastructure to disrupt or destroy another target or produce cascading consequences

Wrong. Terrorists do not need that; all they need is media attention and any explosion with minimum casualties is enough to get it.

5."As security measures around more predictable targets increase, terrorists are likely to shift their focus to less protected targets".

Wrong. We do not have less protected targets in America.

The Commission on Terrorist Attacks Upon the United States (The 9/11Commission) Report
(Analysis)

1. "Terrorism is a tactic used by individuals to kill and destroy."

Wrong. Terrorism is a form of political struggle or political protest, either individual or organized. The 9/11 attack brought a clear message to the US President: stop supporting Israel and leave Saudi Arabia. A suicide bomber, a group member, for example, is a terrorist and a political tool.

2. "Planning does make a difference, identifying where a little money might have a large effect."

Wrong. Impossible. I was a foreign anti-terror group member - planning starts and ends up with money.

3. "We should offer an example of moral leadership in the world."

Wrong. We have nothing to offer.

4. "America's strategy should be a coalition strategy, that includes Muslim nations as partners."

Wrong. We can have certain Muslim leaders as temporary partners, but not nations.

5. "We recommend the establishment of a National Counterterrorism Center (NCTC), built on the foundation of the existing Terrorist Threat Integration Center (TTIC). NCTC should be a center for joint operational planning and joint intelligence, staffed by personnel from the various agencies."

Wrong. A regular bureaucratic trick when they re-name instead of re-forming a system or organization. Besides, there's a trick inside — "various agencies" never send their best officers to other agencies.

6. "The DCI now has at least three jobs. He is expected to manage the loose confederation agencies that is the intelligence community. He is expected to be the analyst in chief for the government, sifting evidence and directly briefing the President as his principal adviser.

Wrong. No DCI (since 2005 - DIN, Director of National Intelligence) has been able to do all three effectively. His position is not political, it's technical. Then, what about Secretary of State as the "analyst in chief" for the government and president's "principal adviser"?

7. "Lead responsibility for directing and executing paramilitary operations, whether clandestine or covert, should shift to the Defense Department. There it should be consolidated with the capabilities for training, direction, and execution of such operations already being developed in the special operations command."

Right. The only professional idea I heard from the government since 9/11.

8. "Congressional oversight for intelligence — and counterterrorism — is now dysfunctional. We have considered various alternatives…"
Wrong. We have no alternatives.

9. "A specialized and integrated national security workforce should be established at the FBI consisting of agents, analysts, linguists, and surveillance specialists who are recruited, trained, rewarded, and retained to ensure the development of an institutional culture combined with a deep expertise in intelligence and national security."
Wrong. America has no professionals with "deep expertise in intelligence and national security" as the 9/11 attack demonstrated.

Bonus
Get Ready For Disaster

What to do first:
- decide where you should meet your household members in case somebody is lost

- make sure everyone knows the address and phone number of your second meeting place

- know all exit routes from your home and neighborhood

- designate an out of state friend or relative that household members can call if separated during disaster

- account for everybody's needs, especially seniors, people with disabilities, and non-English speakers

What to take:
- copies of your ID's in a waterproof and portable container

- extra set of car and house keys

- credit and ATM cards and cash in small bills

- bottled water and non-perishable food such as energy bars

- flashlight, battery-operated radio, extra batteries

- medication for at least one weak

- first-aid kit

- sturdy, comfortable shoes, lightwear raingear, blanket

- child care supplies or other special care items

What to have in your home:
- one gallon of drinking water per person per day

- canned foods and manual can-opener

- first-aid kit, medications and prescriptions

- flashlight, battery-operated radio

- whistle

- iodine tablets or one quart of unscented bleach (for disinfecting water ONLY if directed to do so by health officials) and eyedropper (for adding bleach to water)

- personal hygiene items

- sturdy shoes, heavy gloves, warm clothes, a blanket, lightweight raingear

- extra fire extinguisher, smoke detectors, carbon monoxide detectors

- mobile phone

- child care supplies or other special care items

Be prepared to evacuate:
- if there is time, secure your home: close and lock windows and doors, and unplug appliances before you leave

- remember, evacuation routes change based on the emergency, so stay tuned to the local news

If you are asked to shelter in place:

- go inside your home or the nearest appropriate facility (school, library, church, etc.)

- take shelter in a room that has few doors and windows.

- seal all doors and windows

- turn off all ventilation systems

- do not used the phone – keep the phone line available for emergency calls

- stay tuned to your radio or TV for emergency information and updates

- if you can, try to seek shelter with friends or relatives outside the affected area

Utilities disruptions:
- if you smell gas: do not smoke or light lighter or matches, do not operate any light switches or electrical devices;

- open windows; evacuate immediately and call 911

- if there's a power outage: call your power provider; disconnect or turn off all appliances that would otherwise go on automatically when service is restored. If several appliances start up at once, they may overload the electric circuits; stay indoors if possible. Never touch or go near downed power lines, even if you think they are safe; keep a battery-operated radio on for updates on the restoration process; if you lose power and/or heat in the winter, insulate home as much as possible; do not use generators indoors – without proper ventilation they can create deadly carbon monoxide

Extremely hot weather:
-   stay out of the sun, drink plenty of non-alcoholic, not-caffeinated fluids, consider going to public pools and air-conditioned stores and moles, or cooling centers; never leave children or those who require special care in a parked car

Earthquake:
-   drop to the floor

-   take cover under a solid piece of furniture or next to an interior wall, cover your head and neck with your arms

-   use a doorway for shelter only if it is in close proximity to you and if you know it is a strongly supported

-   stay inside until shaking stops and it is safe to go outside. Research has shown that most injuries occur when people inside buildings attempt to move to a different location inside the building or try to leave

-   DO NOT use the elevators

-   if outdoors: stay there, move away from buildings, streetlights and utility wires. Once in the open, stay there until the shaking stops. The greatest danger exists directly outside buildings, at exits, and alongside exterior walls. Ground movement during an earthquake is seldom the direct cause of death or injury. Most earthquake-related casualties result from collapsing walls, flying glass, and falling objects.

-   if in a moving vehicle: stop as quickly as safety permits and stay in the vehicle. Avoid stopping near or under buildings, trees, overpasses and utility wires. Proceed cautiously once the earthquake has stopped. Avoid roads, bridges or ramps that might have been damaged by the earthquake.

- be prepared for after-shocks, which often follow an earthquake

Flood:
- be aware of streams, drainage channels, canyons, and other areas known to flood suddenly. Flash floods can occur in these areas with or without such typical warnings as rain clouds or heavy rain.

- if you must prepare to evacuate, secure your home, bring in outdoor furniture, move essential items to an upper floor. Turn off utilities at the main switches or valves if instructed to do so, disconnect electrical appliances, do not touch electrical equipment if you are wet or standing in the water.

- if you have to leave your home: do not walk through moving water (six inches of moving water can make you fall). Use a stick to check the firmness of the ground in front of you. Do not drive into flooded areas. If floodwaters rise around your car, abandon the car and move to higher ground if you can do so safely. You and the vehicle can be quickly swept away.

Remember: six inches of water will reach the bottom of most passenger cars causing loss of control and possible stalling. A foot of water will float many vehicles. Two feet of rushing water can carry away most vehicles including sport utility vehicles (SUV's) and pick-ups.

Hurricane
If you live in a mobile home or temporary structure – such shelters are particularly hazardous during hurricanes no matter how well fastened to the ground. If you live in a high-rise building – hurricane winds are stronger at higher elevations. If you live on the coast, on a floodplain, near a river, or on an

inland waterway. If you are unable to evacuate, stay indoors during the hurricane and away from windows and glass doors, close all interior doors, keep curtains and blinds closed, take refuge in a small interior room, closet, or hallway on the lowest level.

Hurricane categories

Category 1, 74-95(MPH) - *Minimal:* unanchored mobile homes, vegetation. - Storm surge: 4-5 feet.

Category 2, 96-110(MPH) - *Moderate:* all mobile homes, roofs, small crafts. - Storm surge: 6-8 feet.

Category 3, 111-130(MPH) - *Extensive:* small buildings, low-lying roads cut-off. - Storm surge: 9-12 feet

Category 4, 131-155(MPH) - *Extreme:* roofs destroyed, trees down, roads cut-off, mobile homes destroyed. Beach homes flooded. - Storm surge: 13-18 feet

Category 5, more than 155(MPH) - *Catastrophic:* most buildings destroyed, vegetation destroyed, - Storm surge: greater than 18 feet

Volcano.
If volcano erupts where you live, follow the evacuation order issued by authorities and evacuate immediately from the volcano area to avoid flying debris, hot gases, lateral blast, and lava flow. Be aware of mudflows – they can move faster than you can walk or run. Look upstream before crossing a bridge, and do not cross the bridge if a mudflow is approaching. Avoid river valleys and low-lying areas. If you have a respiratory ailment, avoid contact with any amount of ash; use a dust mask or hold a damp cloth over your face to help with breathing. Stay away from areas downwind from the volcano to avoid volcanic ash. Stay indoors until the ash has settled unless there is a danger of the roof collapsing. Close doors, windows and all ventilation in the house

(chimney vents, furnaces, air conditioners, fans. Clear heavy ash from flat or low-pitched roofs and rain gutters. Avoid running car or truck engines – driving car stir up volcanic ash that can clog engines, damage moving parts, and stall vehicles. Avoid diving in heavy ash fall unless absolutely required. If you have to drive, keep peed down to 35 MPH or slower.

Tornado

Tornadoes are nature's most violent storms. Spawned from powerful thunderstorms, tornadoes can cause fatalities and devastate neighborhood in seconds. A tornado appears as a rotating, funnel-shaped cloud that extends from a thunderstorm to the ground with whirling winds that can reach 300 MPH. Damage paths can be in excess of 1 mile wide and 50 miles long. Every state is at some risk from this hazard. Tornadoes generally occur near the trailing edge of a thunderstorm.

During tornado go to a pre-designated shelter area such as a safe room, basement, storm cellar, or the lowest building level. If there is no basement, go to the center of an interior room on the lowest level (closet, interior hallway) away from corners, windows, doors and outside walls. Get under a sturdy table and use your arms to protect your head and neck; do not open windows. If you are inside a vehicle, trailer or mobile home, get out immediately and go to the lowest floor of a sturdy, nearby building or a storm shelter. If you are outside with no shelter, lie flat in a nearby ditch and cover your head with your hands. Be aware of the potential for flooding. Do not get under overpass or bridge – you are safer in a low, flat location. Never try to outran tornado in urban or congested areas in a car or truck; instead, leave the vehicle immediately for safe shelter. Watch out for flying debris – they cause most fatalities and injuries.

Tsunami

Tsunamis are a series of enormous waves created by an underwater disturbance such as an earthquake, landslide, volcanic eruption, or meteorite. A tsunami can move hundreds of MPH in the open ocean and smash into land with waves as high as 100 feet or more. The most destructive tsunamis have occurred along the coasts of California, Oregon, Washington, Alaska and Hawaii. Aras are at greater risk if they are less than 25 feet above sea level and within 1 mile of the shoreline. Drowning id the most common cause of death associated with a tsunami. Tsunami waves are very destructive to structures in the run-up zone. Other hazards include flooding, contamination of drinking water, and fires from gas lines or ruptured tanks.

Before and during a tsunami: turn on your radio to learn if there is a tsunami warning if an earthquake occurs and you are in a coastal area. Move inland to higher ground immediately and stay there. Stay away from the beach; never go down to the beach to watch a tsunami come in- if you can see the wave you are too close to escape it ! If there is noticeable recession in water away from the shoreline his is nature's tsunami warning and it should be heeded. You should move away immediately.

Thunderstorm
If you are in the forest, seek shelter in a low area under a thick growth of small trees. In an open area, go to a low place such as a ravine or valley; be alert for flash floods. Go to land and find shelter immediately if you are on the open water. Anywhere you feel your hair stand on end (which indicates that lightning is about to strike), squat low to the ground on the balls of your feet; place your hands over your ears and your head between your knees; make yourself the smallest target possible and minimize your contact with the ground; do not lie flat on the ground.

Building collapses or explosions
- if you are in a building: get out as quickly as possible

- if you can't get out of the building: get under a sturdy table or desk

- if you are trapped by debris: cover your nose and mouth with a cloth or clothing

- move around as little as possible to avoid kicking up dust, which is harmful to inhale; if possible, use a flashlight;

- tap on a pipe or wall so rescuers can hear where you are; shout only as a last resort as shouting can cause you to inhale dangerous amounts of dust

Hazardous materials or chemical spills:
- stay upwind of the material if possible

- seek medical attention as soon as possible if needed

- if there's event indoors, try to get out of the building without passing the contaminated area

- if exposed, remove outer layer of clothes, separate yourself from them, and wash yourself

A parcel or letter may be considered suspicious if there is:
- handwritten or poorly typed address, incorrect titles or titles with no name, or misspelling of common words

- addressed to someone no longer with your organization or not addressed to a specific person

- strange return address or no return address

- marked with restrictions, such as "Personal", "Confidential", or "Do not X-ray"

- excessive postage

- powder on the outside

- unusual weight given its size, lopsided, or oddly shaped

- unusual amount of tape on it

- odors, discoloration or oily stains

If you receive a suspicious package or envelope:
- put it down – preferably on a stable surface

- cover it with an airtight container like a trash can or plastic bag

- call 911 and alert your building's security officials

- alert others to the presence of the package and evacuate the area

- wash your hands with soap and water if you have handed the package

Nuclear power plant emergency
Nuclear power plants use the heat generated from nuclear fission in a contained environment to convert water to steam, which powers generators to produce electricity. They produce about 20% of the nation's power; nearly 3 million Americans live within 10 miles of an operating power plant. Although the construction and operation of these facilities are closely monitored and regulated by the Nuclear Regulatory Commission (NRC), accidents are possible. An accident could result in dangerous levels of radiation that could affect the health and safety of the public living nearby. Local and state governments, federal agencies, and the electric utilities have emergency response plans in the event of a nuclear power plant incident. The plans define two emergency planning zones. One zone covers an area within a 10-mile radius of the plant, where it is possible that people could be harmed by direct radiation exposure. The second zone covers a broader area, usually up to a 50-mile radius from the plant, where radioactive materials could contaminate water supplies, food crops, and livestock.

The potential danger from an accident at a nuclear power plant is exposure to radiation. This exposure could come from the release of radioactive material from the plant into the environment, usually characterized by a plume (cloud-like formation) of radioactive gases and particles. The major hazards to people in the vicinity of the plume are:

- radiation exposure to the body from the cloud and particles deposited on the ground

- inhalation of radioactive materials

- ingestion of radioactive materials

Radioactive materials are composed of atoms that are unstable. An unstable atom gives off its excess energy until it becomes stable. The energy emitted is radiation, and it has a cumulative effect: the longer a person is exposed to radiation, the greater the effect. Terms to help identify a nuclear power plant emergency are:

- notification of unusual event. No radiation leak is expected, no action on your part will be necessary.

- alert. A small problem has occurred, and small amounts of radiation could leak inside the plant. This will not affect you and no action is required.

- site area emergency: area sirens may be sounded ;listen to your radio or TV for safety information

- general emergency. Radiation could leak outside the plant and off the plant site. The sirens will sound. Tune to your local radio or TV for reports. Be prepared to follow instructions promptly.

During a nuclear power plant emergency:
If you are told to evacuate: keep car windows and vents closed; use re-circulating air.
If you are told to remain indoors:

- turn off the air conditioner, ventilation fans, furnace and other air in-takers

- go to a basement or other underground area, if possible

-    do not use the telephone unless absolutely necessary

If you suspect you have been exposed to nuclear radiation:
-    change clothes and shoes

-    put exposed clothing in a plastic bag

-    seal the bag and place it out of the way

-    take a thorough shower

Keep food in covered containers or in the refrigerator (food not previously covered should be washed before being put in to containers).

Nuclear blast
A nuclear blast is an explosion with intense light and heat, a damaging pressure wave, and widespread radioactive material that can contaminate the air, water and ground services for miles around. A nuclear device can range from a weapon carried by an intercontinental missile launched by a hostile nation, to small portable nuclear devise transported by an individual. All nuclear devices cause deadly effects when exploded, including:

-    blinding light

-    intense heat (thermal radiation)

-    initial nuclear radiation

-    blast

-    fires started by the heat pulse

-    secondary fire caused by the destruction

During a nuclear blast:

- if attack warning is issued, take cover as quickly as you can, below ground if possible, and stay there until instructed to do otherwise; listen for official information and follow instructions

- if you are caught outside and unable to get inside immediately: do not look at the flash or fireball – it can blind you; take cover behind anything that might offer protection; lie flat on the ground and cover your head – if the explosion is some distance away, it could take 30 seconds or more for the blast wave to hit; take shelter as soon as you can, even if you are many miles from ground zero where the attack occurred – radioactive fallout can be carried by the wind for hundreds of miles.

Remember the three protective factors: distance, shielding, time.

Radiological dispersion device (RDD)

Terrorist use of an RDD (often called "dirty bomb") is considered far more likely than use of a nuclear explosive device. An RDD combines a conventional explosive device – such as a bomb – with radioactive material. It is designed to scatter dangerous and sub-lethal amounts of radioactive materials over a general area. Such RDDs appeal to terrorists because they require limited technical knowledge to build and deploy compared to a nuclear device. Also, the radioactive materials in RDDs are widely used in medicine, agriculture, industry and research, and are easier to obtain than weapons grade uranium or plutonium.

The primary purpose of terrorist use of an RDD is to cause psychological fear and economic disruption. Some devices could cause fatalities from exposure to radioactive materials. Depending on the speed at which the area of the RDD detonation was evacuated or how successful people were at sheltering-in-place, the number of deaths and injuries from an RDD might not be substantially greater than from a conventional explosion. The size of the affected area and the level of destruction caused by an RDD would depend on the sophistication and size of the conventional bomb, the type of radioactive material used, the quality and quantity of the radioactive material, and the local meteorological conditions – primarily wind and precipitation. The area affected could be placed off-limits to the public for several months during cleanup efforts.

Chemical attack
If you are instructed to remain in your home or office building:
- close doors and windows and turn off all ventilation, including furnaces, air conditioners

- seek shelter in an internal room and take your disaster supplies kit

- seal the room with duct tape and plastic sheeting

- listen to your radio for instructions from authorities

If you are caught in or near a contaminated area, you should:

- move away immediately in a direction upwind of the source

- find a shelter as quickly as possible

Contact the author if you want to support his fight for the U.S. national security. Thank you.
Mikhail Kryzhanovsky.
prof777prof@yahoo.com

www.ingramcontent.com/pod-product-compliance
Lightning Source LLC
Chambersburg PA
CBHW021814270326
41932CB00007B/181